# C. S. Lewis

Twentieth Century Pilgrim

# C. S. LEWIS
## Twentieth Century Pilgrim

Janet Hamilton

MORGAN REYNOLDS PUBLISHING

Greensboro, North Carolina

# WORLD WRITERS

Charles Dickens

Ralph Ellison

Stephen King

Jane Austen

Jonathan Swift

O'Henry

Roald Dahl

Robert Frost

Leo Tolstoy

Zora Neale Hurston

Mark Twain

Mary Shelley

C. S. Lewis

# C. S. Lewis: Twentieth Century Pilgrim

Library of Congress Cataloging-in-Publication Data

Hamilton, Janet.
C. S. Lewis : twentieth century pilgrim / by Janet Hamilton. -- 1st ed.
p. cm.
Includes bibliographical references and index.
ISBN 978-1-59935-112-4 (alk. paper)
1. Lewis, C. S. (Clive Staples), 1898-1963--Juvenile literature. 2.
Authors, English--20th century--Biography--Juvenile literature. 3.
Anglicans--England--Biography--Juvenile literature. 4. Church of
England--Biography--Juvenile literature. 5. Christian
biography--England--Juvenile literature. I. Title.
PR6023.E926Z669 2010
823'.912--dc22
[B]

                                    2009007134

Printed in the United States of America
First Edition

*For my sister Suzanne*

# CONTENTS

Clive Staples Lewis (Courtesy of Time & Life Pictures/Getty Images)

# 1

## Warnie and Jack

In the summer of 1941, when Britain was at one of the darkest points of World War II, an Oxford professor was invited to speak on a British radio show about Christianity. In clear, simple language, he made the case for a moral law that distinguishes between right and wrong, which he claimed was known by all people, even if they didn't follow it. These talks became famous all over England, giving hope to people in a desperate time. The speaker was C. S. Lewis, whose experiences in World War I just two decades earlier had solidified his convictions that God did not exist. Yet now, his view had changed.

Born November 29, 1898, Clive Staples Lewis was three years younger than his brother, Warren. Warren was called Warnie by the family, and when he was four years old, Clive announced that he wanted to be called Jacksie. The nickname stuck, and Clive was called Jacksie, later Jack, for the rest of his life. Jack was a very bright and imaginative boy, and soon he and Warnie were inseparable companions and treated each other as equals.

The Lewis family lived in a house called Dundela Villas in Belfast. One of Jack's strongest memories of this home was a day when Warnie came in and showed Jack a miniature garden he had made in the lid of a cookie tin. He had modeled it after their own garden, using bits of moss and shrubs. When Jack saw it, he felt what he called joy for the first time. It was an experience of seeing something beautiful that made him feel a sort of longing. He would experience this occasionally as he grew up when he saw something beautiful, heard certain music, or read a particular poem, and it was something he learned to seek out.

Jack's father, Albert James Lewis, was a successful solicitor, or lawyer. In 1905, when Jack was six, the Lewis family moved to a larger house near the village of Dundonald, outside of Belfast. Albert and his wife, Flora, called the house Little Lea, and they built it themselves with the idea that Albert would retire there in ten or fifteen years. Albert enjoyed politics and was a good speaker. He was famous in the family for what he called his wheezes, funny stories about things that had happened to him. Jack and Warnie loved listening to these, but they didn't like their father's quick temper.

Their mother, Flora, tended to be more analytical and even-tempered. Her father was an Anglican priest, and she had spent part of her childhood in Rome where her father led a church. She received a bachelor of arts degree from Queens University in Belfast with high marks in geometry, algebra, and logic at a time when it was unusual for a woman to do so. Flora loved to read and write and even published a few items in the local paper.

Both of Jack's parents were voracious readers, and their house was crammed with books. From an early age, reading and writing were favorite pastimes of both Jack and Warnie, and each boy created his own imaginary land. Jack was inspired by Beatrix Potter, the author of *The Tale of Peter Rabbit* and many other books about talking animals, as well as by the tales told to him by his Irish nurse, Lizzie Endicott. He invented Animal-Land, a world populated by what he called *dressed animals*—talking mice and rabbits who hunted for cats instead of giants. Warnie was more interested in modern-day inventions like trains and steamships, and his world was an imaginary India. Eventually their two worlds fused into Boxen, a world of talking animals that had countries, inventions, and politics like those around them in Ireland.

This happy period of Jack's life ended shortly after his ninth birthday, when his mother became ill. On February 15, 1908, she had a surgery that revealed that she had abdominal cancer.

The Lewis family and staff, posing on the steps of Little Lea, Belfast, Northern Ireland, 1905. Front row, left to right, Warnie leaning on post, Jack in dark sailor suit, Leonard Lewis (cousin), and Eileen Lewis (cousin). Second row, left to right, Agnes Young Lewis (aunt), maid, maid, Flora Hamilton Lewis (mother), and Albert Lewis, holding dog Nero. *(Courtesy of The Marion E. Wade Center, Wheaton College)*

Jack prayed that his mother would get better, but Flora grew sicker and weaker over the next several months and died on August 23, 1908, Albert's forty-fifth birthday. She had kept a calendar with a Shakespeare quotation for each day. On August 23, the quote, from the play *King Lear*, was, "Men must endure their going hence."

Jack later wrote, "With my mother's death, all settled happiness, all that was tranquil and reliable, disappeared from my life." His father, whose own father had died about four months before Flora, and who lost his older brother two weeks later, became more emotionally unstable and quick to anger.

Just a few weeks after his mother's death, Jack was sent away to Wynard School, an English boarding school that Warnie had attended and hated for the previous three years. Jack was not quite ten years old.

In early twentieth-century England, it wasn't unusual for a boy of Jack's age to go to boarding school. Boys were commonly sent away as early as age seven, for seven months of the year. It was considered a good way to help them cut ties to their parents, especially their mothers. Schools for boys of this age were called

Young Jacksie wearing a sailor suit and holding a toy
*(Courtesy of The Marion E. Wade Center, Wheaton College)*

preparatory schools. Boys attended them for a few years before moving on to public schools, which were similar to American private schools, that prepared the boys to go on to a university.

Albert and Flora Lewis knew very little about English schools, having grown up in Rome and Ireland, but they had carefully researched preparatory schools when it was time to send Warnie to one. They had originally thought of sending him to Campbell College in Belfast, Ireland. At that time, though, Catholics in Ireland were trying to get Home Rule, the chance to govern themselves separately from England. The resulting conflict created a politically turbulent environment for Irish Protestants (like the Lewises). Albert and Flora's decision to send their sons to Wynard also may have been based on their desire for them to learn English ways and make social contacts in England.

Consequently, Albert wrote to his former headmaster and friend W. T. Kirkpatrick or "Kirk," who agreed with the choice of an English school. This led Albert Lewis to consult an educational agency in London called Gabbitas and Thring, which found students and teachers for British schools. They recommended Wynard School, and the Lewises, without having seen the school, sent Warnie off in May 1905.

Wynard was a small school comprising two houses and twenty students, only eight or nine of whom were boarders. It was run by Robert Capron, who had founded the school in 1881. Jack eventually attended three boarding schools, and hated them all because of their strict regimentation and lack of solitude. For him, Wynard was a nightmare. Capron was an abusive man who treated each boy according to his status in British social hierarchy. Fortunately, Jack's intelligence impressed Capron, but Warnie was frequently picked on. In addition, the school was academically weak. Consequently, both boys' educational progress suffered. Lewis called the chapter in his autobiography about these days "Concentration Camp," and gave the school the fictional name "Belsen" after a real German concentration camp. He and Warnie wrote their father frequent letters begging to come home.

A parent brought a High Court action against Robert Capron because of his abusive policies, and by 1910 the school had dwindled to nine students. Capron wrote to Albert Lewis that he had decided to give up teaching, and in September of that year, Wynard closed its doors. Shortly after, Capron was put into an insane asylum, and he died there eighteen months later. By the time Wynard closed, Warnie had moved on to public school, so Jack, who was now almost twelve, was enrolled in Campbell College in Belfast. There, he had an English master named Lewis Alden, nicknamed Octie, who introduced him to the long narrative poems that Jack loved for the rest of his life. Jack didn't get to stay long at Campbell, though, because in November he was sent home with health problems in his chest and lungs. He was frequently sick during his childhood, and his lung difficulties were no doubt made worse by the fact that he and Warnie had both secretly started smoking.

Jack never minded being sick because it meant a chance to stay home and do the two things he loved most: read and write. He got to enjoy a few months of this before his father decided he was well enough to go away to school again. This time, though, instead of returning to Campbell, he was sent to Cherbourg Preparatory School, a small school near Malvern College, the public school where Warnie was a pupil.

Cherbourg was located in the Midlands of England. The town of Malvern was known as a health resort, especially for those with lung problems.

There were seventeen boys at the school, as well as the headmaster, three assistant masters, and Miss Cowrie, the school matron. For the first time, Jack became somewhat friendly with the other boys at school. It was during his time at Cherbourg that he gave up his religious faith. Jack had been raised as a Christian, attending St. Mark's Church with his family. At Wynard, all the boys had to attend church, and Jack took religion there quite seriously. Even after he prayed that his mother would live and she did not, he still continued to believe in God.

At Cherbourg, however, Jack was moving into his teen years, and he began to question the Christianity he had been taught. He was learning about the ancient Greeks and Romans, and he saw that scholars dismissed their religions as something that the ancient people had believed but that really weren't true. He felt that someday Christianity would be viewed the same way. Also, Miss Cowrie, the matron, was interested in the occult and spirituality, and this had an influence on Jack. He had seen prayer and adherence to Christianity as a burden, and he liked the idea of a spiritual world that didn't make any such demands on him. He wrote that, "little by little, with fluctuations I cannot now trace, I became an apostate, dropping my faith with no sense of loss but with the greatest relief."

At the end of his time at Cherbourg, Jack got sick again and ended up taking his examinations in the school sanatorium. Despite his illness, he did well enough to win a classical scholarship to Malvern College, and in 1913, at age fifteen, he followed Warnie to Malvern. Warnie had excelled at the college, and been popular with the teachers and the other boys. Unfortunately, he was caught smoking before Jack began school there. The headmaster threatened to expel him, but Albert Lewis convinced him to let Warnie finish the term and then withdraw from the school. Warnie left before Jack began and studied with a tutor, his father's old friend, Kirkpatrick.

Jack's experiences at Malvern were a mixture of success and unhappiness. He was highly intellectual, but not at all good at sports— like Warnie and his father, he didn't have a middle joint in either of his thumbs, which made him clumsy at anything using his hands. The social structure at Malvern was similar to other English schools at the time. The younger students, those ages thirteen to fifteen, were expected to do chores at any time of day or night when asked by the seventeen- and eighteen-year-olds. Between these chores and the workload from his classes, Jack was exhausted much of the time. He wrote, "Never, except in the front-line trenches (and not always there) do I remember such aching and continuous weariness as at [Malvern]."

The one place where a student could be safe from being asked to do chores was the library, and Jack sought refuge there whenever he could. He was becoming more aware of his above-average intelligence and began to become something of an intellectual snob, looking down on some of the boys who didn't excel in school as he did. His Latin master, Harry Wakelyn Smith (nicknamed Smugy), was Jack's favorite. He improved Jack's Latin and introduced him to Greek, as well as encouraged him to read poetry on his own, especially Irish poet William Butler Yeats and English poet John Milton.

Jack also discovered the music of Richard Wagner and the Norse myths. Wagner was a German composer whose work in the 1800s included four operas called the Ring Cycle that were based on Norse mythology. These operas and books of the myths, particularly one called *Siegfried and the Twilight of the Gods* illustrated by Arthur Rackham, reawakened the feelings of joy Jack remembered from his childhood.

Jack spent only a year at Malvern before following Warnie's footsteps to study privately with Kirkpatrick, whose nickname was "The Great Knock." Kirkpatrick had helped Warnie, who wasn't much of a student, get admitted to Sandhurst, a military academy in England equivalent to the United States' West Point. Not only had Warnie gotten in, he was ranked twenty-first of 201 applicants.

Jack studied with The Great Knock from September 1914 until April 1917. Before Kirkpatrick took him as a pupil, Albert Lewis had sent him a sample of Jack's work, a translation of Latin poetry. Kirkpatrick wrote back to Albert about the translation, saying, "It is an amazing performance for a boy of his age—indeed a boy of any age. The literary skill is one which practiced masters of the craft might envy."

Jack's time with The Great Knock was his first truly stimulating educational experience and made up for his weak early education. This began the minute Jack met Kirkpatrick when he got off the train in Surrey. He happened to comment to his new teacher that the scenery there was "wilder" than he had expected. Kirkpatrick began to question him relentlessly about what he meant by the word "wild" and how much he knew about the local flora and fauna. When Jack was unable to produce any satisfactory answers, Kirkpatrick concluded by asking, "Do you not see, then, that you had no right to have any opinion whatever on the subject?" It was Jack's first introduction to his new teacher's logic and thinking process, and it pointed out his own weaknesses in those areas.

Under Kirkpatrick's guidance, Jack soon developed skills of logic and debate. Although Kirkpatrick at first thought Jack might study law and later envisioned him as a college professor, Jack was sure he was going to become a poet. In addition to the classics in Greek and Latin that he studied with his tutor, he continued with his passion for Norse mythology. He read as much of it as he could, and listened frequently to Wagner's operas. He even experimented with writing his own stories about the Norse gods.

It was during this time that Jack made the first real friend of his own age. Arthur Greeves had grown up near Little Lea, but Jack and Warnie had never been particularly friendly with him. On one of his visits home from The Great Knock's, Jack heard that Arthur was sick. He went to visit him and found him sitting up in bed reading a book of Norse myths. Both Jack and Arthur were astonished to find another boy who shared this passion, and they became close friends and confidantes.

Books became their most frequent topic of conversation. Beginning with Norse mythology, they soon moved on to other reading. Jack read widely at this time, enjoying popular novels, classic English novels, and the English poets, in addition to the books he read with Kirkpatrick. One day in his book shopping, he picked up an old copy of a book called *Phantastes* by George MacDonald. MacDonald was a nineteenth-century minister whose unorthodox beliefs made it difficult for him to earn a living. He was a prolific writer, producing works of fantasy, novels, and children's books. Like Jack, MacDonald's mother had died when he was a young boy, and this loss affected his writing. For instance, in *Phantastes*, the hero goes on a search in the *Faery* world for the perfect woman. When Jack read about this, it reawakened his own feelings of grief and loss that he had buried at boarding school.

Over the years, MacDonald became one of Jack's biggest literary influences. Although Jack acknowledged that George MacDonald was not a good writer, MacDonald had a gift for conveying important ideas through stories. Through his writing, Jack learned the power of fiction to express great truth. Later, Jack called him his master and wrote, "I know hardly any other writer who seems to be closer or more continually close, to the Spirit of Christ himself."

At the time he read *Phantastes*, though, Jack had no interest in MacDonald's Christianity. The Great Knock, who had been brought up as a Presbyterian, had long since decided that religion was illogical and absurd. Jack, already leaning in that direction, was influenced by Kirkpatrick's beliefs and grew more dismissive of religion.

During the period that Jack studied with The Great Knock, Europe was in turmoil. World War I had started shortly before Jack moved to the Kirkpatricks' house. Warnie, who had finished his studies at Sandhurst, was in the war by November 1914. In 1917, when Jack finished his studies with Kirkpatrick and passed the entrance exams for Oxford University, the war was still raging. It was to have a profound effect on the next few years of his life.

A French assault on German positions, Champagne, France, 1917
*(Courtesy of U.S. Department of Defense, National Archives and Records Administration)*

Keble College, Oxford

# 2

## In the Trenches

In December 1916, Clive Staples "Jack" Lewis took the train to Oxford for his scholarship exam. When he got off the train, he accidentally got off on the wrong side and started walking toward the small, somewhat dingy town of Botley. After about a mile, he realized he was headed in the wrong direction. Turning around, he got his first look at the beautiful city of Oxford, with its ancient buildings and spires reaching toward the sky. From that moment, he considered Oxford home for the rest of his life.

Lewis believed it was important to get into Oxford. He wrote, "I knew very well by now that there was hardly any position in the world save that of a don [professor] in which I was fitted to earn a living, and that I was staking everything on a game in which few won and hundreds lost." Kirkpatrick had written a letter to Lewis's father saying, "you may make a writer or a scholar of him, but you'll not make anything else.

You may make up your mind to *that*." Although Jack didn't see that letter until many years later, he already had a sense that the university was the only place he would feel competent pursuing a career.

Oxford University is the oldest university in the English-speaking world, with a history that goes back to at least the eleventh century. It is set up in a way that is different from universities in the United States. Instead of being accepted to Oxford University, students are accepted to one of the thirty-nine colleges that make up the entire university. Although there are large classes, the majority of work is done with a tutor who supervises each student individually. To get a first, or undergraduate degree, a student needs to pass two examinations. The first is called Honour Moderations, and is taken after the first or second year at Oxford. The second exam is called the Honour School and is taken at the end of the undergraduate course. Students receive first-, second-, or third-class honors based on their performance on this exam.

Lewis's scholarship exam that he took on that first trip to Oxford would determine if he would be admitted to one of the colleges. After taking the exam, Lewis told his father he was sure he had failed. Much to his surprise, he received word shortly before Christmas that he had been accepted to University College. Although he could begin as a student, he still had to take an exam called Responsions, which was designed to prove a basic competency in all academic areas.

Lewis went back to Professor Kirkpatrick for one more term to prepare for the mathematical part of this exam. Math was always a weakness, and all his life he struggled with the simplest math, such as making change when he was shopping. He never managed to pass the math portion of Responsions, and had he not been excused from it after his service in the war, might not have been able to continue at Oxford. Lewis began at Oxford in Trinity term, which began in April 1917. Because of the war, there were only 315 students at Oxford instead of the usual 15,000, and many of these were training to become officers. There were only twelve students at Lewis's college, so he was given a large luxurious room with a grand piano and Persian rugs. Usually the dean of the college made an outline of reading for each student, but Lewis didn't get such an outline: He was already in training for the British army and would soon be going to war.

Lewis was not drafted to serve in the army because he was Irish, but he had volunteered. Although he began his training during his first term at Oxford, he still had plenty of time to enjoy himself, swimming and boating on the river, and of course, reading. This pleasant time lasted only a little more than a month, ending when he was called

Mr. and Mrs. W. T. Kirkpatrick in front of their home in Great Bookham, circa 1920. Kirkpatrick ("The Great Knock") tutored Jack for two years and introduced him to the classics in Greek, Latin, and Italian literature. *(Courtesy of The Marion E. Wade Center, Wheaton College)*

up for service on June 7. Then, he was moved out of his fancy room to Keble College, just up the road from University College, which had been turned into a military barracks.

At Keble, he had to share a room, and the roommate assignments had been made alphabetically. Lewis was placed with Edward Francis Courtenay Moore, known as Paddy. Although the two had been put together by chance, this pairing would have a huge effect on Lewis's life. In his letters home, he initially described Paddy as "childish," but later grew to like him. Paddy was Irish but had lived in Bristol, England, since the age of nine when his parents' marriage had collapsed. Although they had never gotten divorced, his father no longer lived with the family. When Paddy moved to Oxford, his mother, Janie, and twelve-year-old sister, Maureen, moved there, too.

Paddy began inviting Lewis home for visits. Lewis, in turn, would entertain the Moore family at University College, where he had managed to keep his beautiful room. Albert got reports on this growing friendship from both Lewis and Janie Moore. When Lewis wrote at the end of August that he had spent almost a week with the Moores, he added about Paddy's mother, "I like her immensely and thoroughly enjoyed myself." Janie Moore wrote, "Your boy, of course, being Paddy's room mate, we know much better than the others, and he was quite the most popular boy of the party; he is very charming and likeable and won golden opinions from everyone."

At the end of September, Lewis was commissioned as an officer and got almost a month's leave, with the understanding that at the end of the leave he would be sent overseas to fight in the war. He spent nearly all of this leave with the Moores. He caught a cold and Janie Moore nursed him, giving him a feeling of being mothered he hadn't experienced since he was nine. He was growing increasingly fond of Janie Moore and she of him. During this time, Lewis and Paddy, who had been assigned to different regiments, made a pact that if one of them was killed, the other would look after the dead man's parent.

Lewis returned to Belfast on October 12, but was gone again on the eighteenth. He had gotten his orders, earlier than expected, to report to Devonshire to train with his regiment. After less than a month of training, on November 15, he received orders to leave for France in two days. He had a short leave, which he spent with Janie Moore and Maureen, who were now back in Bristol. He telegraphed his father, "Have arrived in Bristol on 48 hours leave. Report Southampton Saturday, can you come Bristol? If so, meet at station. Reply Mrs. Moore's address 56 Ravenswood Road Redlands Bristol." His father wired back, "Don't understand telegram. Please write." By the time Albert got a response from Lewis, he was in France. Since Southampton was well known as the departure point for soldiers going to France, Lewis couldn't figure out what had confused his father about his telegram, and the incident further damaged their relationship, already strained since the death of Lewis's mother and his father's temperamental nature.

When Lewis arrived in France, the Allied forces (the British, French, and their allies) had been locked in trench warfare with the Germans and their allies for two years. At the beginning of the war, the Germans had invaded France and tried to take Paris, but had been driven back to northeastern France. The two armies were deadlocked along an area that spread for 450 miles across Belgium and France. This area was called the western front; the eastern front was in Russia, where Germany was also fighting.

Each army had dug a series of trenches six to eight feet deep along the western front from which they could launch their attacks. Although the front was long, it wasn't very deep, and there were towns just a couple miles away that not only survived, but profited from the soldiers who came there. Every few days men would rotate from the trenches to one of these towns, where they could get some rest before going back to fight. Trenches were rat-infested and often wet. The smell of dead bodies filled the air, and there was always the possibility of being killed instantly by a sniper.

Lewis arrived at the western front on November 29, 1917, his nineteenth birthday. He was stationed in Arras, France, where a bloody battle had taken place in April 1917 that had ended in the usual stalemate. By November, the French were refusing to take part in any more of these huge and pointless battles, so there was no major action. At first,

British trench near the Albert-Bapaume Road at Ovillers-la-Boisselle, July 1916, during the Battle of the Somme. (Courtesy of the Imperial War Museum, United Kingdom Government)

Lewis's letters home described the trenches as being not so bad, with time to read and men whose company he enjoyed. Soon, however, he was writing about the sounds of shells flying overhead and the deaths of some of the men.

In February 1918 Lewis had what was considered the good fortune to contract trench fever. This illness, similar to influenza, was spread by lice in the trenches. During World War I, more men were in military hospitals for trench fever than for wounds. Lewis was taken to a military hospital in Le Treport, France, located on the English Channel. He stayed there for about a month, and enjoyed spending the time in bed, reading by the sea. Warnie, who was stationed fifty miles away, made the one hundred-mile round trip on a bicycle in one day to visit.

That spring the Germans were starting to step up their attacks. The Russian Revolution had taken place, and the Germans had begun peace talks with Vladimir Lenin, the new leader of Russia. German soldiers could be brought from the eastern front to the western front. On the other hand, a British blockade of Germany had left the German people almost starving. Plus, the United States entered the war in April, greatly increasing the manpower

Vladimir Lenin

available to the Allies. The Germans knew they couldn't stay in the war much longer, so they began a push for a quick victory.

On the Allied side, every man who could carry a gun in the trenches was needed. Lewis was sent back to the front on March 21. Less than a month later, on April 15, he was wounded in the Battle of Arras. He was with his sergeant, Harry Ayres, and a good friend, Laurence Johnson, when a British shell that had fallen short exploded behind them. The other two men were killed, and Lewis was hit by shrapnel in the hand, the upper leg, and under the arm. Pieces of the shrapnel, which broke a rib and entered his left lung, remained in his chest for the rest of his life.

He was taken to a mobile army hospital in Etaples, France, again on the English Channel but farther north than he had been in Le Treport. Albert Lewis contacted Warnie to tell him Lewis was seriously hurt, and sent Warnie to visit. Warnie was relieved to find that Lewis was doing well, and sent a letter to their father reprimanding him for causing him so much worry.

Although he would recover from his wounds, Lewis was out of action for the rest of the war.

In May, Lewis was sent to Endsleigh Palace Hospital in London, then to a convalescent home in Bristol a month later. He wrote several letters to his father asking him to come visit, but Albert stayed in Ireland. First he had bronchitis, but even after he was well he didn't make the trip. Warnie believed this was because Albert hated breaking his routine and leaving his work, but their father was also drinking heavily by this time, which may have been a factor as well. Whatever the reason, Albert's behavior fueled Lewis's growing resentment.

Janie Moore, on the other hand, was a frequent visitor. She and

Lewis had corresponded several times a week during his time in France. She had received word that her son Paddy was missing, and learned in September 1918 that he was dead. When Lewis was released from the hospital to a convalescent home in July, he chose to stay at the Moores' house in Bristol. He was there until October, and during this time he and Janie grew even closer.

Despite the twenty-five year difference in their ages, the two of them felt drawn together. They had both grown up in County Armagh, Ireland, and both had lost parents at an early age. Lewis's early loss of his mother may have influenced his attraction to Janie, and the loss of her son probably affected her feelings for Lewis. During their years together, he called her Mother and she sometimes called him "Boysie."

Lewis was always extremely private about his relationship with Janie. In describing his life at Oxford in his autobiography, Lewis wrote, "I must warn the reader that one huge and complex episode will be omitted. I have no choice about this reticence. All I can or need to say is that my earlier hostility to the emotions was very fully and variously avenged." Early on in his relationship with Janie, Lewis had written to Arthur Greeves that he loved somebody, but this was apparently the only time he ever made such an admission. Any attempts made by his father or Warnie to find out about his feelings toward Janie Moore were stonewalled, causing both men to worry about Lewis's growing involvement with a much older, still-married woman.

Warnie grew increasingly hostile toward Janie, feeling that she had stolen Lewis away from his own family. His feelings grew stronger several years later when he moved in with the couple. He wrote, "The thing most puzzling . . . [was Mrs. Moore's] extreme unsuitability as a companion for him. She was a woman of very limited mind, and notably domineering and possessive by temperament." On the other hand, Owen Barfield, a friend since Lewis's early Oxford days, considered Janie Moore to be extremely solicitous of Lewis, to the point of spoiling him.

When he was a student at Oxford, relationships with women were strictly forbidden, and he risked being suspended if anyone there found out about Janie. Even after his student days were over, he remained private about the relationship, so that even his closest friends weren't sure about it. What is known is that they became close during this time at the end of the war.

Though many friends and biographers have speculated, no one knows for sure if Lewis and Janie Moore had a strictly platonic relationship. Owen Barfield once said he thought there was a fifty-fifty chance that Lewis and Janie Moore had a sexual relationship. Maureen Moore recalled that when she was growing up, Lewis and her mother insisted that she go to church every Sunday morning, even though neither of them showed any inclination toward attending. As she got older, she realized that they just wanted her out of the house to give them a rare opportunity to be alone together.

In November 1918, World War I ended. Lewis still had military obligations and was unable to get leave at Christmas. On Christmas Eve, he unexpectedly learned that he had been discharged and immediately headed for Belfast, where Warnie was spending his first Christmas at Little Lea since 1913. He arrived on December 27, much to the surprise of Albert and Warnie. Despite the strained relationship between Lewis and his father, and despite the fact that Albert had never visited Lewis when he was injured, the three of them enjoyed the visit. Warnie wrote

Queens College, Belfast

in his diary, "It was as if an evil dream of four years had passed away and we were still in the year 1915."

Although Lewis rarely spoke about his time in the war, occasional allusions indicate that his war experiences haunted him for years to come. In a letter to his father at the end of the war, he mentioned that he was physically feeling good, but that he was having "nightmares—or rather the same nightmare over and over again." Twenty years later, when a friend wrote and asked if he would be joining the Territorials (a volunteer reserve army designed to defend England in the event of a German invasion), he wrote, "I am too old. It w[oul]d be hypocrisy to say that I regret this. My memories of the last war haunted my dreams for years."

One particularly difficult aspect of the war for Lewis was that he felt he was losing the imaginary worlds he had learned about through literature, worlds he loved as a child and adolescent. Still, he had continued writing during his time in the army, and had completed a book of poems called *Spirits in Prison*. In September 1919, the book was accepted for publication by Heinemann Publishers. The publisher changed the title, and the book appeared as *Spirits in Bondage* by Clive Hamilton. This was a remarkable achievement for Lewis, who turned twenty-one that November.

When Lewis was asked once by a friend if he had been frightened during his time in the trenches of France, he answered, "All the time, but I never sank so low as to pray." In spite of this statement, many of his poems written during the war had references to God, usually expressing anger that he couldn't sense God's presence or that God didn't exist.

In addition, the poems in *Spirits in Bondage* frequently mentioned the magical world of his imagination, but again, usually in the context that it no longer existed:

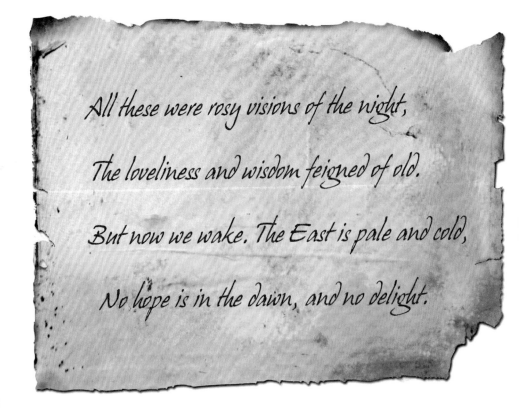

All these were rosy visions of the night,

The loveliness and wisdom feigned of old.

But now we wake. The East is pale and cold,

No hope is in the dawn, and no delight.

Lewis once said that during his adolescence, "nearly all that I loved I believed to be imaginary; nearly all that I believed to be real I thought grim and meaningless." His poetry from the war revealed his fear that his imaginative half was dying. It was also revelaed that he was angry about losing the joy that had been so important to him in his childhood.

The Radcliffe Camera at Oxford. The circular library holds books from the Bodleian Library's English, history, and theology collections.

# 3

## Scholar

In January 1919, after a two-week visit with his father and brother, Lewis finally returned to Oxford as a student at University College. He was given the same luxurious rooms he'd had before the war, and resumed his studies of classical literature. He was excused from the Responsions exam because of his war service, and could also have skipped the Honour Moderations or "Mods," which covered Greek and Latin literature, but he was advised that he should take this exam since he wanted to have an academic career. He spent the next year preparing for it. Lewis didn't find these studies too difficult since he had already read and enjoyed most of the material while studying under Kirkpatrick.

At Oxford, Lewis came to appreciate more fully the joys of friendship. As a child, he and Warnie had been so close that they didn't like having interruptions from other boys. "Our lives were already full, and the holidays too short for all the reading, writing, playing, cycling, and

Jack and Warnie, in Annagassan, 1949
(Courtesy of The Marion E. Wade Center, Wheaton College)

talking that we wanted to get through. We resented the appearance of a third party as an infuriating interruption." While he had enjoyed a close friendship with Arthur Greeves, their relationship consisted mostly of written correspondence.

During the war, Lewis had become close friends with Laurence Johnson, one of the soldiers killed by the same shell that had wounded Lewis. Before the war, Johnson had been a student at Queens College in Oxford, and Lewis had enjoyed lively debates with him during their times away from the front. Now Lewis sought to find other friends like Johnson at Oxford, and he was not disappointed. He joined a debate society called the Martlets, which met once a week. Lewis enjoyed the gatherings and was soon elected secretary.

At Oxford, Lewis decided to adopt what he called "The New Look." This had nothing to do with his physical appearance, but with his intellectual outlook. He wrote that he decided there would be "no more pessimism, no more self-pity, no flirtations with any idea of the supernatural, no romantic delusions." He no longer sought out what he had called joy, dismissing it for the most part as an aesthetic experience he had in the past.

One of Lewis's closest friends at Oxford was Owen Barfield, a brilliant scholar who remained a lifelong friend. Lewis called Barfield his "Second Friend." He believed that a First Friend was the friend with whom you shared your views and was like an alter ego (Arthur Greeves in his case), while a Second Friend was one with whom you disagreed on most issues and could enjoy debate and discussion. Lewis said about the Second Friend, "He has read all the right books but has got the wrong thing out of every one. It is as if he spoke your language but mispronounced it. How can he be so nearly right and yet, invariably, just not right?"

Although Barfield had been raised in a household without much religion, during his years at Oxford he embraced a philosophy called Anthroposophism, which included a belief in God. This appalled Lewis and marked the beginning of what the two men came to refer to as their "Great War." While Lewis never embraced the same philosophies as Owen, their arguments at Oxford and their correspondence forced Lewis to re-examine and solidify many of his ideas and opinions. One idea he changed almost right away due to Barfield's influence was what he called chronological snobbery. This was a belief that contemporary ideas were better than those of the past. Barfield got him to see that while some beliefs were no longer accepted because they had been proven wrong, others had simply gone out of style. This included ideas about religion.

Despite a busy schedule of academics and time with friends, Lewis had not forgotten Janie Moore. She and Maureen had moved to the city of Oxford, and Lewis rode his bike to their house for a visit every day at one in the afternoon. He had to be extremely secretive about these visits. Marriage for Oxford dons had only been permitted in the previous generation or two, and student relationships with women were severely frowned upon. If his association with Janie Moore had been discovered, it would have probably excluded Lewis from ever pursuing a career as an Oxford don.

This was not the only strain put on Lewis by his relationship with Moore. She could be quite demanding and bossy, frequently asking Lewis to help her around the house and to run errands, which cut into the time he could spend on his studies. Lewis was also helping her financially, since payments from her estranged husband were irregular. Since Lewis was living on an allowance intended to support a single person, this put a strain on his finances. Lewis couldn't possibly ask his father for additional funds, since he was trying to keep Janie Moore as much of a secret as possible from both Albert and Warnie.

Lewis returned to Ireland for the summer, but living with his father proved to be difficult. Tensions simmered until one day Albert confronted Lewis about his finances, and Lewis assured him they were fine. His father then produced a bank statement he had found that said that Lewis's account was overdrawn. Albert was angry with Lewis for lying, while Lewis was furious at his father for snooping, and told him he had lost all respect for him. After a major argument, Lewis returned to the Moores' home before the summer break was over.

Second-year Oxford students were expected to move out of college rooms and find rented rooms, so Lewis decided to stay at the Moores' house for the school year. This made secrecy much more difficult, and resulted in what would be the lowest point in his relationship with Warnie. Warnie refused to come to the Moores' house and would only meet Lewis on neutral ground, such as a restaurant or pub. In addition, Warnie was developing more orthodox Christian beliefs while Lewis's beliefs were moving further in the opposite direction. Warnie also had begun drinking heavily.

Despite the difficulties in his private life, Lewis continued to perform brilliantly in his academic work. In the spring of 1920, near the end of his second year at Oxford, he took the Honours Moderations exams and was placed in the First Class with the highest First. For this honor, he received a prize of five pounds to spend on books. A year later, in the spring of 1921, he won the Chancellor's English Essay prize for an essay on Optimism, which he was required to read before all the dignitaries of Oxford. Shortly after this presentation, William Kirkpatrick, his former tutor, died. Lewis felt the loss deeply. None of his Oxford tutors had made as much of an impression or had as much of an influence on him as The Great Knock had.

Although Lewis had excelled at English, and was still writing poetry (he was working on a long mythical poem called *Dymer*), his academic pursuits were leaning toward philosophy, and he envisioned himself becoming a philosophy professor. Most of his friends, including Owen Barfield, were poets or loved poetry, and English literature seemed to be Lewis's natural preference; Kirkpatrick had felt it was his greatest strength. But he was drawn toward philosophy, in part because of his sense, strengthened by his war experiences, that he was losing his imaginative side. Perhaps Lewis believed that studying philosophy would strengthen the rational, logical part of himself. He may also have been discouraged by the lack of recognition that came from the publication of *Spirits in Bondage*.

In the summer of 1922, he received a First Class degree in what was commonly called Greats. The full name was Honours School of Literae Humaniores, and it was a degree in Greek and Latin Language and Literature combined with Ancient Philosophy and Ancient History. He now had a Double First, the mark of a true academic.

This degree was the equivalent of an undergraduate degree, and it qualified him to begin looking for a job as a university don. Although he wanted to stay at Oxford, most Oxford dons began their careers at different universities. Lewis had a couple of offers, but didn't feel he could accept them because of his ties to the Moores, whom he either wanted to stay with or have them accompany him. He was offered a job in the classics department at Reading University, but this was too far away for Maureen Moore to continue to attend Headington School for Girls in Oxford. He also had the opportunity to take a one-year position at Cornell University in Ithaca, New York, but he would have had to come up with travel expenses, and again, he was reluctant to leave Janie Moore.

Although Lewis hated to continue his dependence on his father, he felt he had no choice but to accept when Albert offered to keep supporting him until a position as an Oxford don became available. During his final term at Oxford, he had had an interview with the Master of University College, who encouraged Lewis to stay at the college an extra year and get a degree in English. He decided to pursue this during 1922-1923.

At this time, English was a relatively new academic field, considered to be not quite as scholarly as history, philosophy, and the classics (Greek and Latin literature). Oxford had recently had a royal commission evaluate its curriculum, with the results made public in the newspaper. Their finding was that the popularity of the classics was waning, while

English was rising. Although English had been taught for only about thirty years at Oxford, many students were interested in it, and it seemed like a more promising field for Lewis to pursue than philosophy or classics. In addition, the curriculum included much of the literature that Lewis had always loved and that had nurtured his imagination.

During his undergraduate days, Lewis's closest friends had been from other colleges. Now, while studying English, he found friends among his classmates. One man who remained a lifelong friend was Nevill Coghill, a fellow Irishman who had also fought in the war. Much to Lewis's surprise, he learned that Coghill was a member of the Church of Ireland and a believer in Christianity. Like Arthur Greeves and Owen Barfield, here was another man who shared many of Lewis's interests

Magdelen College tower

and passions and who also believed in the existence of God and another world.

In addition to this disturbing (to him) trend among his friends, Lewis began to notice that almost all the writers who spoke to him most profoundly were Christians or had some sort of religious beliefs. The Christians included George MacDonald, the fantasy writer he had discovered during his days with Kirkpatrick, as well as G. K. Chesterton and the poets John Milton and Edmund Spenser. The most religious ancient writers like Plato, Aeschylus, and Virgil were also his favorites. On the other hand, he found nonbelieving writers he read, such as H. G. Wells, George Bernard Shaw, and Voltaire, to be entertaining but somewhat shallow.

A darker experience during this year caused Lewis to continue to adhere to his "New Look," despite the beliefs of his friends and favorite writers. Janie's brother, Dr. John Askins, lived

Engraving of Voltaire at age seventy, from 1843 edition of his *Philosophical Dictionary*.

just outside Oxford, and had a friendly relationship with Lewis. Neither Lewis nor Janie realized that Dr. Askins was suffering from syphilis, a disease that eventually affected his brain. He became convinced that demons were speaking to him and that he was soon going to die and go to hell. The doctor and his family moved into Janie Moore's house while they waited for an opening at an insane asylum. For two weeks, Lewis helped care for him during periods where he had screaming fits and had to be sedated with chloroform. Askins had always been interested in the supernatural and had explored spiritualism, theosophy (a study of the cosmos and deities believed to bring more wisdom than traditional religion), and yoga. To Lewis, Askins's madness was a warning to stay away from such pursuits and remain in the world of the rational and concrete.

At the end of his additional year at Oxford, Lewis got another First in English, and was back to looking for a job. He learned that E. F. Carritt, an Oxford don who had been his philosophy tutor, was going to America for a year, which meant that University College needed a substitute. Lewis was hired to take Carritt's place as a philosophy don for one year. Philosophy at this time was considered a scientific study in which questions of religion were considered meaningless and not worth pursuing. This was in contrast with Lewis's recent English studies. Again, the struggle between the rigorous logical side and the imaginative part of Lewis's nature was at work, with logic winning out once more.

This temporary teaching position relieved some of his financial concerns, although Albert continued to supplement his income with an allowance. In April 1925 Lewis heard about and applied for a position as an English don at Magdalen College at Oxford. Initially, he believed that he didn't have much hope of getting the position, but soon learned that he was one of two finalists for the job. The position was for a man who could help with teaching philosophy, which of course made Lewis a strong candidate. He and his rival John Bryson were invited to a formal dinner with the Magdalen faculty to allow the dons to assess their manner and conversation. Afterward, Lewis was elected to join the faculty of one of the largest and most beautiful colleges at Oxford.

When he learned the good news, one of Lewis's first actions was to send his father a telegram that read simply, "Elected fellow Magdalen. Jack." He soon followed it up with this letter:

First, let me thank you from the bottom of my heart for the generous support, extended over six years, which alone has enabled me to hang on till this. In the long course I have seen men at least my equals in ability and qualifications fall out for the lack of it. "How long can I afford to wait" was everybody's question: and few had those at their back who were both able and willing to keep them in the field so long. You have waited, not only without complaint but full of encouragement, while chance after chance slipped away and when the goal receded furthest from sight.

Thank you again and again.

This letter marked the end of Lewis's financial dependence on Albert, and with it a relaxation of some of the tensions between them. While Lewis would never really love or feel affection for his father, from then on they were able to visit with each other without the arguments and strain that had marked Lewis's student years. When Lewis visited Albert in Belfast that October, Albert wrote in his diary, "Very pleasant, not a cloud."

Magdalen College, Oxford

# 4

## Reluctant Convert

C. S. Lewis began his career as a don of Magdalen College in the summer of 1925, at the age of twenty-six. Magdalen is considered one of the most beautiful colleges at Oxford, consisting of more than one hundred acres of land that includes a deer park and part of the river Cherwell running through it. Lewis was given rooms at the college, which included a sitting room and a bedroom. He expected the rooms to be furnished but discovered that they weren't, and immediately had to pay about ninety pounds (the equivalent of four thousand pounds today) to get himself some furniture. His salary at this time was five hundred pounds a year, up from his father's allowance of 210 pounds.

Less than a century before Lewis moved to Magdalen, Oxford dons had been required to remain unmarried and celibate. Although this was no longer a rule, most of them in the 1920s were single and lived in their rooms at the college. Even those who were married ate their meals in the college's dining hall. Lewis followed this tradition, living in his rooms and eating with the other dons, although he still visited the Moores' house almost every afternoon during the school terms, and slept there on the weekends and during holidays. He would work there during the vacations between terms, despite Janie Moore constantly interrupting him to do domestic chores for her. "Minto," as Lewis now called Janie, developed a series of illnesses, possibly psychosomatic, that kept Lewis waiting on her. When Lewis was working, she was quite protective of him. She shielded him from others who might interrupt him, but was never hesitant to make frequent demands on him herself. She was now fifty-three, and her daughter Maureen was nineteen.

As the English don at Magdalen, Lewis was responsible for preparing all the English students in the college for their degrees. He was involved with the administration of the college as well, but his main duties involved teaching. He gave a lecture about once a week, but spent most of his teaching time meeting individually with students in tutorials. In the typical Oxford fashion, his students would have a weekly reading assignment, from which they would prepare a 3,000-word essay. This essay would then be discussed and debated with Lewis at their weekly tutorial, where students got input on their essays and also learned to defend their positions. At the beginning of his time at Magdalen, Lewis also taught philosophy and traveled once a week to Lady Margaret Hall, a women's college in North Oxford, to teach a class there.

A typical day for Lewis at Magdalen started early in the morning with a servant arriving at his rooms to bring hot water, prepare his shaving kit, and empty his chamber pot (there were no indoor bathrooms for the college rooms). This servant also cleaned his rooms daily.

Breakfast was at eight, served in what was called the Senior Commons Room where all the Magdalen dons ate morning and midday meals. This was Lewis's favorite meal, and he always arrived for it promptly. Breakfast was a time when Lewis would talk to the other dons or glance through the *London Times*, although he was never too interested in events of the day. Following breakfast, he took a walk, then began his tutorials around nine. He would have two or three meetings in the morning, with a thirty-minute break between each one.

In the afternoon, Lewis sometimes delivered a lecture. If none was scheduled, he spent the time reading, evaluating students' essays, doing administrative work, or preparing for upcoming lectures or tutorials. Dons dressed up for dinner, which was called High Table. It was a five-course meal with any liquor available upon request for the dons or their guests. Following the meal, everyone went to the Senior Commons Room for "wines," which was a time for discussion and more drinking. During his early career, Lewis began aging quite a bit; he lost much of his hair and gained weight, which was undoubtedly due in large part to his lifestyle as a don.

Jack Lewis in the "little end room" at Little Lea, Belfast, Northern Ireland, December 1919. *(Courtesy of The Marion E. Wade Center, Wheaton College)*

As he became accustomed to his new career, Lewis found that he liked some aspects of it better than others. He found the work of a tutor tedious at times. Since he was teaching the same literature to each student, he had to discuss the same works several times each week—and then do that again the following year and the year after that. Having been a gifted student himself, he sometimes expected too much from his students, and he would become irritated or frustrated with those who were less than brilliant. He could be particularly unsympathetic to students who considered themselves privileged or expected to coast through because of their wealth. He was more patient with those who were hardworking and respectful, even if they were not academically talented. Later in his career, he used humor to disguise his irritation at those who weren't as bright as he was, and he learned to soften his style of argument. Not surprisingly, this made him much more popular as a tutor.

As a lecturer, he was quite different from most of his contemporaries at Oxford in the 1920s and 1930s. He disliked answering students' questions before or after a lecture, particularly after his popular books made him famous. He usually arrived about five minutes late for a lecture and would start talking right away, sometimes even beginning in the hallway outside the classroom. He would begin leaving the lecture room as he was finishing up, and would deliver his last sentence while walking out the door. Again, he enjoyed using humor and anecdotes to keep his lectures interesting, and was particularly good at using everyday explanations and metaphors to help explain difficult concepts. In spite of his jokes and down-to-earth style, his lectures were packed with information, all delivered in a slow, deep voice, often slowing down to dictation speed if he was quoting an author he didn't want his audience to miss.

Although his academic career kept him busy, Lewis hadn't given up his dream of being a poet. He had been working on his epic poem *Dymer* since the end of the war, and he completed it in the spring of 1926. Although Lewis claimed his poem was not at all autobiographical, it is difficult to believe it was not influenced by his relationships with his father and Janie Moore. It tells the heroic journeys of Dymer, a young man who starts out by escaping The Perfect City, which combined all the things Lewis hated about his schools and the army, with leaders maintaining order through strict conformity and rules. He meets an older woman who is at first beautiful, but later turns into an ugly and demanding hag. Dymer believes that if he is slavishly devoted to her, she will eventually return to her beautiful state, but she never does. The two of them have a child together who turns out to be a monster. The monster kills his father, Dymer, who then goes to heaven where both he and the child become gods.

Jack showed *Dymer* to Nevill Coghill, a friend from his undergraduate days, who was now a don on the English faculty of Essex College, another Oxford college. Coghill liked it very much and sent it to Dent, a publishing company. *Dymer* was published by Dent under the name Clive Hamilton in September 1926, the beginning of Lewis's second year at Magdalen. Every week, Lewis would check the London *Times Literary Supplement* for a review of *Dymer*, but none appeared for almost a year. When the review was finally published, it was positive, but it was too late to have any impact on sales, and the book was considered a failure. For the most part, this put an end to Lewis's dreams of being a poet, and he seldom attempted to write poetry after *Dymer*.

Lewis had used the support of colleagues at Oxford to help write and publish *Dymer*. They had given him encouragement and feedback about his writing, and Nevill Coghill had been instrumental in helping him get it published. This set a pattern that continued for the rest of Lewis's life. He always surrounded himself with intellectual friends who enjoyed listening to and critiquing one another's work.

Although Lewis was popular with the faculty during his early years at Magdalen, he was disappointed with the clubs he found there. There were quite a few, but most were based on shared interests in sports or politics, both of which Lewis disliked, and lacked the kind of intellectual conversation that he loved. He soon formed his own club called Beer and Beowulf, which met once a week in his rooms. The Beowulf part of the name comes from an epic poem written in England during the Middle Ages, the only surviving epic from the Anglo-Saxon period of English history. As the name of the club suggested, the main activities at meetings were drinking and discussing Old English literature.

Lewis found more friends among the English faculty of other Oxford colleges. In the spring of 1926, Lewis met another don who was to become an important friend in his life. John Ronald Reuel (J. R. R.) Tolkien had been appointed Rawlinson and Bosworth Professor of Anglo-Saxon at Pembroke College at the same time Lewis had begun at Magdalen. Although Tolkien was living a more conventional domestic life than Lewis—he was married and would eventually have four children—the two men had much in common. Like Lewis, Tolkien had fought in the trenches during World War I and contracted trench fever. Both had lost their mothers at an early age (Mabel Tolkien had died at age thirty-four when her son was twelve), had strong links to their childhoods, loved fantasy literature, and were interested in expanding their careers as writers. They were both far more interested in their intellectual fields than in any contemporary events.

The monogram and estate trademark of J. R. R. Tolkien

Tolkien had a deep interest in the language and stories of Old English. The first time he and Lewis met was at a meeting of the English faculty, in which Tolkien was proposing a change to the English curriculum to eliminate all literature from 1830 onward so that they could focus more on Old and Middle English (a move Lewis opposed). After an early meeting, Lewis wrote about Tolkien in his diary, "He is a smooth, pale, fluent little chap . . . thinks all literature is written for the amusement of men between thirty and forty. . . . No harm in him: only needs a good smack or two."

Lewis came to change his first impressions completely, and within a few months of meeting, the two men were getting together frequently in Lewis's rooms to discuss literature and history, and to review each other's manuscripts. Tolkien invited Lewis, Nevill Coghill, and some other Oxford dons to join a group he had formed to read Norse myths in the original Icelandic language. The group was called the Coalbiters from the Icelandic word *kolbiter*, meaning those who get so close to the fire in winter they bite coal. Although Lewis didn't speak or read the language they were studying, he had learned from Professor Kirkpatrick to plunge into reading a new language, and was soon reading his beloved Norse myths in their original Icelandic.

Tolkien was a devout Catholic. His mother had converted to Catholicism against the strong objections of her Baptist family, and this influenced him in his faith all his life. Lewis was acutely aware that most of his friends were believers of some sort. Nevill Coghill and Lewis's old friend Owen Barfield were both Theists, which meant they believed in God, although they didn't consider themselves Christians. Lewis's childhood friend Arthur Greeves had been a Christian for quite a while, and they frequently discussed religion and philosophy in their letters.

During this period, Lewis was reading much of the work of G. K. Chesterton, a contemporary British writer who argued that the love of story is closely connected to the Christian faith. Chesterton argued that the greatest stories are those that express our deepest experiences. One of Chesterton's books that most influenced Lewis was *The Everlasting Man*, a history of humankind told from a Christian perspective. This book was written partly in response to another book, *Outline of History* by H. G. Wells, in which Wells wrote of man from an evolutionary point of view, arguing that he was simply another animal and that Christ had been merely a human with great influence. Lewis, having always admired Chesterton's work, was affected by the fact that he could write about history from a religious perspective.

Another literary work that had a profound effect on him at this time was a Greek play called *Hippolytus* by Euripides. For no particular reason, Lewis felt compelled to reread this play, and was drawn to one of the choruses that included a lot of imagery about the world's end. The next day he found himself overwhelmed by the feelings this passage had provoked, and he wrote, "the long inhibition was over, the dry desert lay

*The Death of Hippolytus*, an 1860 painting by Sir Lawrence Alma-Tadema

behind, I was off once more into the land of longing, my heart at once broken and exalted as it had never been since the old days."

During the summer of 1929, Lewis began to feel as if God was approaching him. Slowly during the past decade, he had felt the influence of his friends and favorite writers who believed in God. He had even gone so far as to acknowledge an absolute spirit in the universe, although he still separated this from any God of religion. Emotionally, he had left behind his decision to be purely rational.

One day, Lewis was riding a bus in Oxford when he became aware that he was keeping something shut in, or perhaps shut out. He described it as a feeling that he was wearing tight clothing or a suit of armor, and he realized he had a choice of keeping this clothing on or shedding it. Although he felt as though he had a free choice, it seemed impossible to him not to make the decision to open the door, and so he did. Immediately, he wrote, "I felt as if I were a man of snow at long last beginning to melt. The melting was starting in my back—drip-drip and presently trickle-trickle. I rather disliked the feeling."

This experience marked the beginning of a period during which Lewis felt he was being relentlessly pursued by God, no matter how he tried to cling to his logical doubts about God's existence. Although he felt himself drawing closer to belief, he was still afraid of what this would mean in his life, and of the emotions it might unleash in him. Finally, he could no longer resist acknowledging his belief in God. He wrote, "You must picture me alone in that room in Magdalen, night after night, feeling whenever my mind lifted even for a second from my work, the steady, unrelenting approach of Him whom I so earnestly desired not to meet. That which I greatly feared had at last come upon me. In the Trinity Term of 1929 I gave in, and admitted that God was God, and knelt and prayed: perhaps, that night, the most dejected and reluctant convert in all England." Lewis now believed in God and would steadfastly maintain that faith for the rest of his life.

At the end of the summer, Lewis went through another life-altering experience: the illness and death of his father. Albert Lewis had retired in May 1928 at the age of sixty-five, and his health had begun to decline almost immediately. In late July, Lewis received a letter from his uncle Dick telling him that his father was losing weight and having frequent, severe intestinal pain. Lewis went home for a visit on August 13 and realized that Albert was very sick. Warnie had been sent to Shanghai, China, for a tour of duty, so he was unable to get home to help out, and letters from Ireland to China took several weeks to reach their destination.

Lewis ended up staying in Ireland for more than a month, nursing his father. Their relationship was at its most harmonious, although Lewis was still haunted by memories of past conflicts and angry partings from his father.

In early September, Albert went into a nursing home and had abdominal surgery, which revealed that he had colon cancer. He seemed to improve after the surgery, and the doctors told Lewis that it was possible his father would live for a few more years. With his work piling up at Oxford, Lewis left Belfast on September 21, only to receive a telegram on the twenty-fifth that his father had taken a turn for the worse. He was on a train an hour later, but by the time he arrived his father was dead.

Warnie didn't receive the letter about Albert's death until October. Both men were upset not only by the loss of their father, but about losing their childhood home as well. When Warnie was able to get home in April 1930, he and Lewis went about disposing of the contents of the home and selling the house. Warnie was about to retire from the army, and Lewis was planning to use the proceeds from the sale to buy a house in Oxford that could be shared by Warnie, Janie Moore, Maureen, and himself. Getting rid of the remnants of their childhood was extremely emotional for the brothers, who both still had strong links to their early life at Little Lea. Warnie wanted to save their toys and preserve them in a special room in the new house, but Lewis talked him out of it. In the end, they buried a trunk filled with characters from Animal-Land in the vegetable garden and sold or gave away the rest.

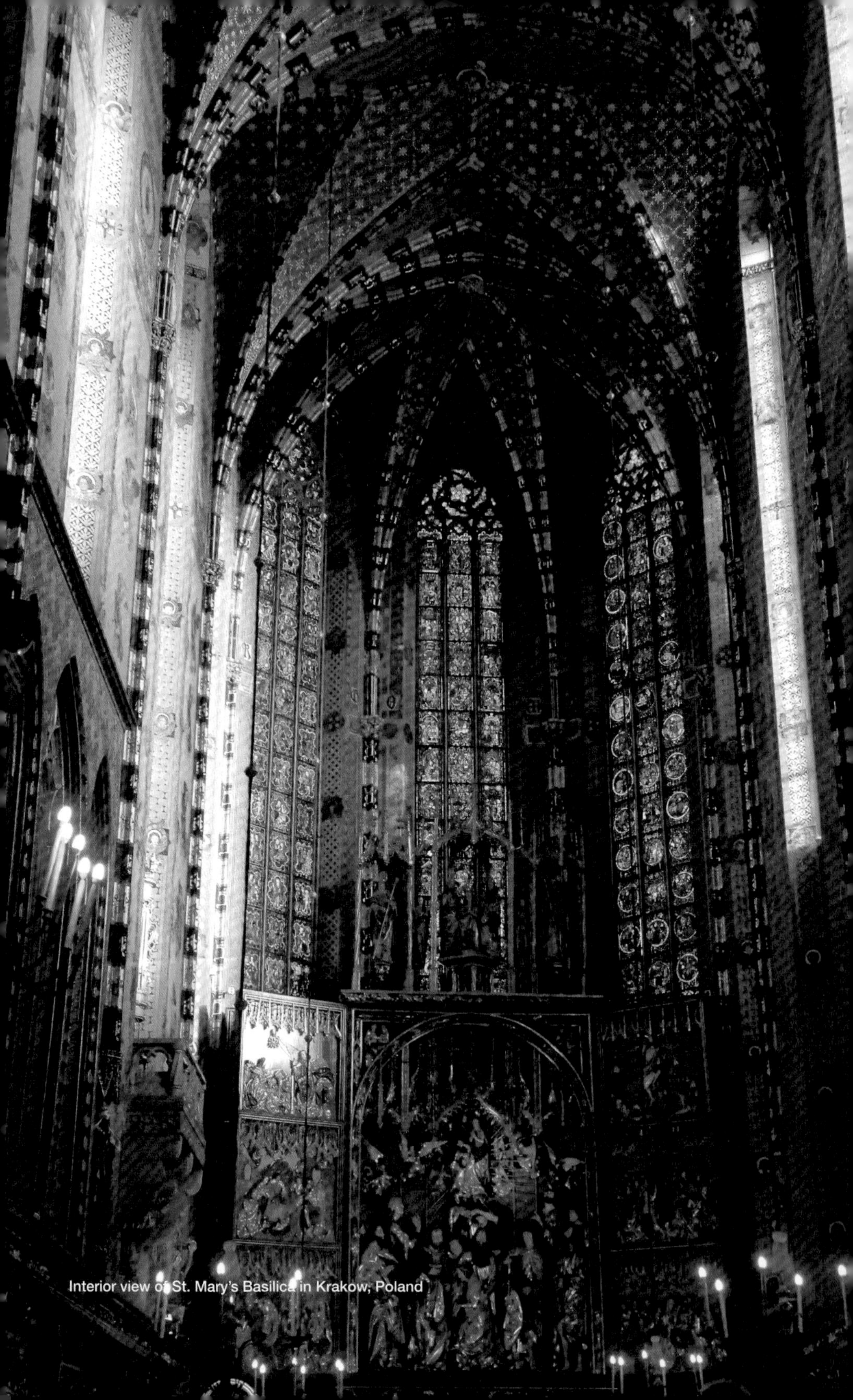

Interior view of St. Mary's Basilica in Krakow, Poland

# 5

## Write Some Ourselves

Lewis's religious conversion and the death of his father marked the beginning of the most creative period in his life. During the next two decades he hit his stride as a writer, producing many books, both scholarly and popular. His writing was deeply influenced by his religious beliefs, starting with his acceptance of God, and continuing with his later conversion to Christianity. This was also a period in which friendships became more important to him than ever, both as a person and as a writer.

This era in Lewis's life began with the realization of his dream of buying a house for himself, Warnie, and the Moores. Although he had some money from the sale of his father's house, and Janie Moore and Warnie contributed as well, it was not easy to find a house in Oxford that they could afford. They finally found a place that they liked, a fairly small cottage on a large plot of land. It was the land that sold both Lewis and Warnie on the property—eight acres that were surrounded by woods and included a pond. The house was called the Kilns, named for two old brick kilns that stood next to the house.

During the three eight-week terms of school at Oxford, Lewis continued to live at his rooms in Magdalen, although he visited the Kilns almost every day and spent weekends there. He usually got a ride home at lunchtime from Maureen or Frank Paxford, a gloomy gardener who worked at the Kilns. Warnie had retired from the army in 1932 at the age of thirty-five and moved into the new house. This created a new tension in the household, since Warnie and Janie never got along very well. Since Warnie had a pension from the army, he didn't need to work, and he never really figured out what to do with his life. This lack of purpose led to an increase in his drinking. Always attached to his childhood, Warnie began a project of organizing all the Lewis family papers and putting them into chronological order. This ended up taking years, and later on he wrote two books about the history of France. He frequently worked on these projects in Lewis's rooms in Magdalen. Students who came for tutorials grew accustomed to walking past him as he worked at his typewriter.

Lewis and J. R. R. Tolkien continued their friendship and spent many hours in each other's rooms, reading their works in progress and discussing literature and religion. Tolkien was Catholic, while Lewis now believed in God but couldn't quite bring himself to embrace Christianity. Since his conversion in 1929, he had started attending chapel every day at Oxford and going to his local parish church on Sundays. This was not because he considered himself a Christian, but because he felt he should show some sign to the world that he was now a believer.

Church to him was more of a duty than something he enjoyed. He disliked the aspect of gathering together with a large group of people and the endless organization of church work. He never grew to enjoy the musical part of the church service, claiming that the organ was his least favorite instrument. In addition, he wrote that he still felt sometimes that his prayers were like "posting letters to a non-existent address," and described his religion as "not precisely Christianity, tho' it may turn out that way in the end."

In a typical fashion, Lewis began an intellectual analysis of the world's major religions. Having studied mythology extensively, he thought he saw hints given in the myths of other cultures about the truth about God. He began to believe that Christianity was unique in that it contained elements of both history and mythology that he couldn't find in any other religion. Christ had been a historical figure, but his story also contained the mythology of the dying god that Lewis had read about in other myths.

An important conversation with Tolkien in September 1931 moved him closer to accepting Christianity. Lewis had invited Tolkien to dinner at Magdalen along with Henry "Hugo" Dyson, a friend who was an English lecturer at Reading University, as well as a Christian. After dinner, the three of them went for a walk around the grounds of Magdalen and started debating the truth of Christianity. Lewis talked about how he saw the story of Jesus's death and resurrection as a myth, similar to the myths he had loved since childhood, such as the story of the Norse god Balder who dies and later is resurrected.

Tolkien also had been passionately interested in mythology for many years and had thought a great deal about its connection with Christianity.

He believed that myths were stories that revealed spiritual truth. He also believed that the story of Jesus, the Christian "myth," was different from all other myths because it really happened. They went back and forth on these topics until Tolkien finally left at three in the morning; Dyson and Lewis continued talking for another hour.

This conversation was pivotal in helping Lewis move from believing in God to fully embracing the doctrine of Christianity. Nine days later, on September 28, 1931, he went on a trip to the Whipsnade Zoo with Janie, Maureen, and Warnie. Warnie drove his motorcycle and Jack rode with him in the sidecar. This ride proved to be as momentous as his bus trip two years earlier when he felt like he had shed a tight suit of clothing. He wrote, "When we set out I did not believe that Jesus Christ is the Son of God, and when we reached the zoo I did. Yet I had not exactly spent the journey in thought. Nor in great emotion. . . . It was

more like when a man, after long sleep, still lying motionless in bed, becomes aware that he is now awake." Like his experience on the bus, he became aware of a feeling and made a choice based on this feeling, this time choosing to accept that Jesus Christ was the son of God.

On October 1, he wrote to Arthur Greeves, "I have just passed on from believing in God to definitely believing in Christ—in Christianity. I will try to explain this another time." On October 18, he wrote a longer explanation, detailing his conversation with Tolkien and Dyson, but this time he ended, "Does this amount to a belief in Christianity?" Although he still felt some questions and doubts, from then on he considered himself a Christian.

Lewis's Christianity had an almost immediate impact on his writing. At the beginning of 1932, he told Warnie that he wanted to write a long poem about man's search for joy. In August of that year, he took a vacation at Arthur's house in Ireland, not far from where his own childhood search for joy had begun. In two weeks, he wrote *The Pilgrim's Regress*, the story of a man named John who leaves his home in a country called Puritania because he is afraid of the powerful Landlord there. After many travels, he returns home and discovers that the Landlord (God) is a kind guide, not a tyrant. The story, which Lewis used to describe his own spiritual journey, was based on the seventeenth-century book *The Pilgrim's Progress* by John Bunyan, about a man's journey from earth to heaven.

Although the main focus of his book was spiritual, Lewis also used it to satirize some contemporary writers and politicians. Initially, *The Pilgrim's Regress* sold only 650 copies. Some reviewers thought Lewis was Catholic, and a Catholic publisher, Sheed and Ward, issued a new edition of the book in 1935, which sold an additional 1,500 copies.

Lewis wrote another book about Christianity during this time called *The Problem of Pain*. A man named Ashley Sampson, who owned a small London publishing house, was putting together a series called "Christian Challenge," and he asked Lewis to contribute a 40,000-word entry to the series. The book Lewis wrote was on human suffering and a Christian perspective on how a loving and powerful God can allow pain and suffering. It looks at how God uses pain to create more perfect human beings.

Another book by Lewis appeared in 1935, this one a scholarly work titled *The Allegory of Love* that established his reputation in the area of medieval literature. The book had taken Lewis ten years to write, beginning in 1925, when he first had the idea of writing a complete history of how love is represented in writings from ancient Rome to the end of the sixteenth century. This book had an enormous effect on the study of literature. For instance, the sixteenth-century poet Edmund Spenser, whose poem *The Faerie Queene* is now considered an important contribution to English literature, had been almost completely forgotten until Lewis devoted a chapter to him in *The Allegory of Love*. Lewis's work is still considered the most important book on love literature from the sixth to the sixteenth centuries. Not only did it establish Lewis as an important scholar in his field, but in this book he found the voice he would use in his future writing—warm, inviting, and accessible, making the material understandable to many readers.

Publication of this book led Lewis to a man who became another influential friend. Charles Williams was an editor at Oxford University Press who read the manuscript, and soon after received a fan letter from Lewis about Williams's novel, *The Place of the Lion*. Williams had just written to Lewis praising *The Allegory of Love*; the letters crossed in the mail. They began a correspondence that grew into a close friendship. Williams was different from some of Lewis's other friends. He was self-educated, having had to leave University College of London due to financial difficulties. A spiritual person who considered himself a Christian, Williams was also fascinated by the occult. He wrote scholarly works about literature, as well as poetry and fantasy novels that were called "supernatural thrillers." Although Williams lived in London, he occasionally visited Lewis in Oxford.

For his next book, Lewis moved to a completely different genre. This book began with a conversation he had with Tolkien about fantasy literature in which Lewis commented, "There is too little of what we really like in stories. I am afraid we shall have to try and write some ourselves." They agreed that Tolkien should write a time-travel story and Lewis would try his hand at science fiction. The results show the extreme differences in the two men's writing styles. Lewis was a quick writer who rarely revised, whereas Tolkien was painstakingly slow, frequently looking back to the mythology that was so much a part of his writing. He began a time-travel story called *The Lost Road*, his only story that took place in contemporary times, but he never finished it. He had recently published the critically acclaimed book *The Hobbit*, and was much more interested in working on the sequel, which became *The Lord of the Rings* twelve years later.

Lewis, on the other hand, quickly dashed off his science-fiction book, which he called *Out of the Silent Planet*. Although he was somewhat influenced by science-fiction writers Jules Verne and H. G. Wells, his book was more allegorical and included very little science. It's the story of a man named Elwin Ransom who is kidnapped by two sinister men going to the planet Mars, called Malacandra in the story, which they have visited before. Because they believe the planet's inhabitants eat people, they take along Ransom as an extra human to feed to the Martians. Once there, Ransom manages to escape and learns that Malacandra, as well as all the other planets in the universe except Earth, are ruled by angel-like creatures called eldila, and that the residents are peaceful and loving. Earth, known as the silent planet, has fallen and is no longer under the care of Maledil, the god of the universe, but instead is controlled by a devil-like figure. Lewis eventually continued Ransom's story in two more books, *Perelandra* and *That Hideous Strength*.

Lewis read each chapter of *Out of the Silent Planet* aloud to a group of friends that included Tolkien. Once he had finished, he sent it to the publisher of his poem *Dymer*, who turned it down. Tolkien sent it to Allen and Unwin, Ltd., the publishers of *The Hobbit*. While the editors there decided not to publish it, they sent it to a small publishing company called The Bodley Head who accepted it. *Out of the Silent Planet* sold

Victoria Crater, Mars, as seen by Nasa's Mars Exploration Rover *(Courtesy of NASA)*

better than any of Lewis's other books so far.

By this time, the literary gatherings of the Coalbiters had stopped meeting, but soon a new group formed to take its place. Lewis and Tolkien were invited to a meeting of a dining club called the Inklings, organized by an Oxford undergraduate named Edward Tangye Lean for the purpose of sharing and critiquing writing. When Lean graduated in 1933, the club broke up, but Lewis took over its name and moved the meetings to his college rooms at Magdalen. It's not clear why the name Inklings was originally chosen, but Tolkien said about it, "It was a pleasantly ingenious pun in its way, suggesting people with vague or half-formed intimations and ideas plus those who dabble in ink."

The Inklings began meeting on Thursday evenings and eventually expanded to Tuesday morning meetings as well. The Thursday gatherings were generally in Lewis's rooms and were for sharing and critiquing the members' writing, while the Tuesday group met at a pub called The Eagle and Child (nicknamed The Bird and Baby) and were given to more general discussion.

Regulars included Lewis, Tolkien, Hugo Dyson, Nevill Coghill, Owen Barfield, Warnie, and a doctor friend named Robert Havard who was always known as Humphrey, after one of the members accidentally called him that, or the UQ (Useless Quack). Charles Williams was an occasional visitor and became a regular after he moved to Oxford during World War II. Others were occasionally invited to join if Lewis met someone he felt fit the criteria for membership: a man who was a good conversationalist, maintained an interest or involvement in writing, and enjoyed drinking.

Although Lewis had a great many friends, he did not get along with his colleagues at Magdalen as well as he had at the beginning of his career. Many of them disapproved of his science-fiction book, which they considered not scholarly enough for an Oxford don. In 1938, Lewis further alienated some of the dons with a prank that got out of control.

One morning, Adam Fox, the chaplain at Magdalen and a friend of Lewis's, read in the paper that a man named Edmund Chambers had been nominated for a position at Magdalen called the Professor of Poetry. This professor, instead of being hired by the college, was elected every five years by dons and former students of the university. Although Chambers was a published poet with a great deal of knowledge about sixteenth-century poetry, Fox and Lewis knew little about him and believed he was an inappropriate choice for the job. Fox remarked, "This is simply shocking, they might as well make me Professor of Poetry," to which Lewis replied, "We will." Lewis took it upon himself to begin a campaign for Fox, complete with slogans and meetings with voters.

Meanwhile, those who supported Chambers grew worried because Fox was a popular figure whom they thought might win the election.

They put up a third candidate, Lord David Cecil, a friend of Lewis's and an occasional visitor to the Inklings meetings. Cecil and Chambers split the opposition vote, which allowed Fox to win and become Professor of Poetry. He ended up doing a mediocre job, and Lewis later admitted that it had been a mistake to give him the position. In addition, he had alienated many of the dons at Magdalen, which ended up hurting his career later on.

# 6

## Speaker of Faith

On September 30, 1939, England and France declared war on Germany, and World War II began in Europe. Lewis wrote about the beginning of the war, "If its got to be, its got to be. But the flesh is weak and selfish and I think death would be much better than to live through another war." To Arthur, he wrote, "What makes it worse is the ghostly feeling that it has all happened before—that one fell asleep during the last war and had a delightful dream and has now waked up again." Yet in spite of his dread of another war, the years of World War II, from 1939 until 1945, proved to be some of the most productive and happiest of Lewis's adult life.

The war brought changes in Lewis's household and within his circle of friends. Warnie was called back to active service in the army and sent first to Yorkshire, England, and then to France in early 1940. He spent several months there, in and out of military hospitals being treated for alcohol-related illnesses. In May 1940, he was evacuated from France during the Battle of Dunkirk, and returned to the Kilns in August.

Lewis feared briefly that he too might be drafted for military service. In 1939, the British government set the age range for eligibility from eighteen to forty-one. Since his forty-first birthday was in November 1939, Lewis could have been called up. However, given his limited military experience and unfit, overweight physical condition, he never was. Instead, he volunteered to serve with the Oxford City Home Guard Battalion, as did many other Oxford academics, including J. R. R. Tolkien.

The Battalion's job was to patrol a designated area of the city of Oxford once a week from 1:30 a.m. until 5:30 a.m. Usually Lewis would go after a late-night Inklings meeting. Although he eventually found this duty tiresome, he enjoyed the quiet early-morning hours. During this time he wrote some of the pieces that later appeared in his book, *The Screwtape Letters*, whose main character is an air raid warden during World War II.

This book was written as a series of letters between a junior devil, named Wormwood, and Screwtape, a senior devil who is training Wormwood to do evil and tempt humans. It first appeared as installments in a weekly Anglican magazine called *The Guardian* between May and November 1941. Ashley Sampson, who had commissioned Lewis to write *The Problem of Pain*, convinced his publisher to publish *The Screwtape Letters* as a book, and it came out in February 1942. The original 2,000 copies sold out almost immediately, and the book, which has been in print ever since, has sold more than a million copies. Although this book made C. S. Lewis a household name, it did not make him wealthy, since he donated all the proceeds from it to charity.

One of the issues Lewis reflects on in this book is how the war might cause a person to grow in virtue or fall into sin. When Wormwood expresses happiness that the war has begun, Screwtape cautions him that it might not have the effect he assumes. "Of course a war is entertaining. The immediate fear and suffering of the humans is a legitimate and pleasing refreshment for our myriads of toiling workers. But what permanent good does it do us unless we make use of it for bringing souls to our father below?" He goes on to say that people might "have their attention diverted from themselves to values and causes which they believe to be higher than the self." Lewis saw this as a potential positive effect of the war and worked to do what he could to encourage people to turn to Christianity during wartime.

*The Screwtape Letters* led to a new opportunity to reach people all over Great Britain. The Royal Air Force (RAF) chaplains invited Lewis to do a series of lectures to soldiers at stations around the country. His speeches gave a Christian perspective to simple topics such as, "Why We Think There Is a Right and Wrong." James Welch, an Anglican priest who had left his parish to become the Director of Religious Broadcasting at the BBC (British Broadcasting Corporation), heard about the talks that Lewis was doing for the RAF, and had read *The Screwtape Letters*. Believing that the BBC had a patriotic duty to supply spiritual and moral support to the British during wartime, Welch invited Lewis to do a series of radio broadcasts similar to his RAF talks.

Lewis began these broadcasts on August 6, 1941. He would travel by train from Oxford to London each Wednesday evening and do a live performance from seven forty-five until eight o'clock, then return

home on the late train. He proved to have a gift for radio broadcasting, with a breezy, self-confident voice and a conciseness in delivery. He mostly focused on Christian behavior, attempting to answer such questions as, "Can an intelligent person be a Christian?" and, "What should a Christian's attitudes be toward money? Or war?" The talks were collected and published as three books: *Broadcast Talks* in 1942, *Christian Behaviour* in 1943, and *Beyond Personality* in 1944.

These books were eventually combined into one volume called *Mere Christianity*. The title came from the work of Richard Baxter, a seventeenth-century writer who lived in England during a time of civil war. One group of Christians, the Puritans, supported Parliament, and another group, the High Church Anglicans, supported the king. Although Baxter was a Puritan, he didn't like the idea of sects or divisions within Christianity. He felt that Christians were united by more ideas than those that divided them, and he said he was a "Mere Christian."

Lewis frequently made similar arguments, encouraging Christians to focus on Christianity rather than its separate denominations.

Lewis was asked to do more broadcasts, but he never did. For one thing, he felt he had said what he wanted to say and didn't want to start repeating topics. He also disliked all forms of popular culture, and only did the radio programs because he felt it was his Christian calling to try to reach a wide audience. In addition, he could not keep up with the volume of mail his radio programs and books were generating.

Lewis received letters of support from England and abroad, particularly from the United States. Lewis felt that since he was expressing his ideas publicly, it was his duty to answer all the letters people wrote him as a result. Many of the initial letters turned into lengthy correspondences; for instance, during the 1950s he wrote 138 letters to an American woman who mostly complained about the sinful nature of her family members. Eventually, Warnie devoted much of his time to helping Lewis with his letter writing. Often Lewis would write an outline that Warnie would turn into a full letter. In addition to the toll all of this took on Lewis's time, the postage was also a considerable financial expense. Since he donated the proceeds from his talks and *The Screwtape Letters* to charity, Lewis was still living mostly on his salary as an Oxford don.

Besides his nonfiction books, Lewis continued the science-fiction series he had begun with *Out of the Silent Planet*. During the early 1940s he completed the other two volumes of the trilogy, *Perelandra*, published in 1943, and *That Hideous Strength*, which came out in 1946. *Perelandra* takes its name from the residents' name for the planet Venus, where the story takes place. Ransom, the protagonist of *Out of the Silent Planet*, meets a woman named Eve who is being tempted by his old enemy Weston. Ransom acts to save Eve, and in the process saves Perelandra from a fall similar to Adam and Eve's fall that led people on Earth to sin.

The third installment, *That Hideous Strength,* is twice as long as the other two books and was greatly influenced by the work of Lewis's friend, Charles Williams. Unlike the other two, it takes place on Earth, in a small university town. The evil National Institute for Coordinated Experiments (N.I.C.E.) is trying to cause the downfall of humanity through the main character, Mark Studdock, and his wife, Jane. Ransom enlists the help of the wizard Merlin to rescue Mark and Jane, and in the process, all of humanity. Lewis's negative portrait of the professors at N.I.C.E. reflected his own feelings about some of his Oxford colleagues. This further alienated him from the other dons at Oxford, many of whom already looked down on much of his writing. They didn't feel it was proper for an Oxford don to write science-fiction novels and popular books about religion.

In spite of these differences, Lewis was still focused on his academic career. In 1943, he published a book called *A Preface to Paradise Lost,* which was based on a series of lectures about John Milton's epic poem, *Paradise Lost.* Published in 1667, *Paradise Lost* is the story of Adam and Eve's fall. It focuses on Satan, portayed in the story as a fallen angel who tempts Adam and Eve as revenge against God for expelling him from Heaven. Lewis's lectures and subsequent book analyzed the sources and influences for *Paradise Lost*, and looked at its impact on writers who came after Milton. As usual, Lewis's work was impeccably researched and accessible to readers, written in an intelligent, conversational tone.

Another area of interest at Oxford was the Socratic Club, an organization that began as an undergraduate debating club. One week a Christian would present a paper and a non-Christian would respond; the next week the roles were reversed, with questions and debate from the other members encouraged. The club was started by a former student named Stella Aldwinckle who had studied theology at Somerville College at Oxford in the 1930s. Since all undergraduate clubs had to have a senior member, she invited Lewis to join in 1941. Within a few months, he became president and rarely missed a meeting until he left the post in 1954.

While Lewis was productive during the war years, his home life was becoming increasingly difficult. As Janie Moore grew older, she became more demanding, expecting Lewis to stop his work and take care of domestic chores whenever she called for him. Her daughter Maureen got married in October 1940, which meant that she was out of the house and no longer available to help. Fortunately, in 1943, someone else came in who more than took her place.

Since the beginning of the war, children had come to stay at the Kilns for various periods of time because they had to be evacuated from homes that were in danger of being bombed. One of these evacuees was June Flewett, a sixteen-year-old who came to stay during the summer of 1943. She was a devout Catholic who had read many of Lewis's books, although she didn't realize who he was when they first met. At first she thought he and Warnie were Janie's sons, and she was impressed by Lewis's kindness and devotion to Janie. While the other young people who came to stay at the Kilns only remained a short while, June was happy there and ended up staying for the next two years. Lewis felt it was not the best environment for a young girl, and finally convinced her to study at the Royal Academy of Dramatic Arts in 1945. This was a sad parting on all sides; not only had Lewis, Warnie, and Janie all become very fond of June, but her departure meant the full burden of the household chores came back to Warnie and especially to Lewis.

Lewis still maintained his many friendships, although many of them changed during the war years. The Oxford University Press moved from London to the relative safety of Oxford, which meant that Charles Williams was now living nearby. Lewis helped him get a position as a lecturer on the English faculty at Oxford, and he became popular with students. The two men became closer friends and, in some ways, Williams replaced Tolkien in Lewis's affections.

Although Lewis still considered Tolkien a friend, their differences began to become more apparent. Tolkien, who was Catholic, disapproved of Lewis's religious writings. He felt that only the clergy should instruct people on religion. While Lewis enjoyed spending time with a variety of friends, Tolkien had always preferred the time he and Lewis spent alone. Tolkien was not as fond of Charles Williams as Lewis was, and this strained their friendship as well. Nevertheless, they continued their relationship and still enjoyed sharing their literary works in progress. Tolkien was continuing work on his masterpiece, *Lord of the Rings*. He was a slow, deliberate writer who would spend a long time on a single passage. This was a contrast to Lewis, who wrote quickly and did little revising of his work. Lewis liked *Lord of the Rings* a great deal and continually encouraged Tolkien to keep moving ahead on it.

On May 8, 1945, the war in Europe ended. The next day Charles Williams was suddenly taken to the hospital with stomach pain and

Man mourning at graveyard

underwent an operation a few weeks later, on the evening of June 14. When Lewis went to visit him the next morning, he learned that Williams had died a few hours earlier. Lewis was devastated. In a letter, he referred to Williams as his "dearest friend." Despite his grief, he felt that Williams was still close. He claimed that he felt his friend's presence at his funeral, and that this sensation made the journey to "the next world" seem more real.

In December 1945, there was an Inklings gathering, partly to celebrate the end of the war and partly to remember Charles Williams. The Lewis brothers, Tolkien, and Robert Havard met at a small village in Gloucestershire for a few days of walking and gathering in pubs. At the end of it, Warnie recorded in his diary, "As if our holiday had intended to end then, the sky clouded over and the world became dim: the curtain had fallen most dramatically on our jaunt."

Merton College Chapel

# 7

## Chronicles

Although the war years had been difficult in England, they were a time of great personal and public success for Lewis. During this time, his friendships flourished, he became world famous for his talks and writings on Christianity, and he saw his career at Oxford going well. The years immediately following the end of the war proved to be much more difficult for him.

Lewis began to realize how much his popular writings had hurt his career at Oxford. For a while, Lewis and Tolkien had both had their eyes on the two English chairs at Merton College. These were positions in which they would become professors with no tutorial duties—their only responsibilities would be lecturing, supervising graduate students, and helping to run the college. Tolkien told his son Christopher that it was his ambition to move to the Merton Chair of English Language and see Lewis get the Merton Chair of English Literature. Tolkien got his wish when he got the language chair in 1945. Two years later, David Nicholl Smith, the occupant of the other chair, retired, and both Tolkien and Lewis believed that Lewis would be chosen to replace him.

Unfortunately, they underestimated the degree of dislike for Lewis held by his colleagues. While Lewis had published excellent scholarly works, such as *The Allegory of Love* and *A Preface to Paradise Lost*, these accomplishments were overshadowed in the dons' estimation by his more popular works. Although many of these men were Christians, they believed it was not proper for a professor to write about Christianity the way Lewis did. They also felt these books, as well as his science-fiction works, were not scholarly enough to reflect well on an Oxford don.

In addition, many of his colleagues saw Lewis as argumentative and opinionated. Some still remembered his belligerent campaign to elect Adam Fox as Professor of Poetry. Although Lewis was often described as kind, he also had sharp verbal skills that he used against people if he felt the occasion called for it. Robert Havard, his physician and friend, said of Lewis, "He could be intolerant, he could be abusive, and he made enemies." In the end, these enemies prevented him from becoming a professor at Oxford. F. P. Wilson got the Merton Chair of English Literature professorship.

Lewis got one more chance for a professorship, this time the Professor of Poetry position that had gotten him into trouble many years before. Unlike the Merton Chair, which is a position appointed by the Oxford dons, the Professor of Poetry is elected every five years, and anyone who has received a degree from Oxford can vote on it. In 1951, Lewis was nominated to run against poet Cecil Day-Lewis. Despite a vigorous campaign run by his friends at Oxford, he lost the election by twenty-one votes. This time, Lewis was less disappointed than those who ran the campaign for him. It's possible he was not particularly interested in the position, and ran more for the sake of his friends than for himself.

In 1947, Lewis published another book on Christianity entitled *Miracles*, which makes a case for a benevolent being, God, who is responsible for the existence of miracles. Lewis felt it was essential for a person to choose whether or not the world can be perceived merely through the senses, or if there is a larger supernatural universe. This book became the topic for a debate at the Socratic Club in early 1948. A young philosophy don named Elizabeth Anscombe was invited to debate Lewis about the third chapter of *Miracles*. Anscombe was a follower of Ludwig Wittgenstein, a contemporary philosopher. Although she was a Catholic, she felt that Lewis's arguments in this particular chapter didn't stand up to current philosophy.

For the first time, Lewis was completely defeated in a debate. While observers that night agreed that he was defeated, they disagreed on the result of this defeat. Some felt that he was so devastated by the defeat that it caused him to stop writing the sorts of books he had written up to that point. While many of the books he wrote after the debate reflected on Christianity in various ways, Lewis never again wrote using his intellectual skills to defend Christianity like he had in *Mere Christianity* and *Miracles*. Some felt this was because he no longer thought his beliefs could stand up to rigorous debate.

Others disagreed. While it's true that his next work was The Chronicles of Narnia, a fantasy series written for children, there were a number of other factors influencing his decision to move in that direction. Lewis acknowledged that Anscombe was very bright, commenting to his friend Havard, "Of course, she is far more intelligent than either of us." He ended up revising chapter three of *Miracles* in later editions, based on the arguments she had made in their debate.

In addition to these professional difficulties for Lewis, he was feeling increasing stress over the situation at the Kilns. Janie Moore was growing more and more difficult to care for. Due to ulcerated varicose veins in her legs, she had been a semi-invalid for several years. During the war, June Flewett had been there to take on many of the domestic tasks, but June had left in January 1945, when Lewis paid her expenses at the Royal Academy for the Dramatic Arts for two years, and she became a successful actress. A succession of maids were hired after she left, but none was ever satisfactory to Janie. Maureen and her husband lived close by, but they rarely visited.

Meanwhile, Warnie's drinking was growing steadily worse, and he and Janie increasingly irritated each other. He often escaped to Ireland, where he could drink without criticism from Lewis or Janie. In addition, Janie began suffering from dementia, which made her obsess over household chores, particularly walking her elderly dog, Bruce. She wanted him to be walked ten or more times a day, a task that, like many others, fell mostly to Lewis. In June 1949, Lewis collapsed from exhaustion, suffering from swollen glands and a high fever. Dr. Havard put him in the hospital, fearing that his condition was serious for a man over fifty who was overweight and out of shape. Warnie railed against Janie to stop nagging Lewis so much about household responsibilities. He then went on a drinking binge that brought on a temporary psychosis

An 1873 illustration of Daniel in the lion's den, from the biblical Book of Daniel

and landed him briefly in a mental hospital. In April 1950, Janie's doctor had her moved to Restholme, a nursing home in Oxford. She was suffering from advanced dementia and had repeatedly fallen out of bed. Lewis visited her there every day, and worried that he wouldn't be able to pay for her care if she lived past his retirement. She died on January 12, 1951, with Lewis at her side.

On the day of her death, Warnie wrote in his diary, "And so ends the mysterious self imposed slavery in which J has lived for at least thirty years. How it began I suppose I shall never know." The relationship between Lewis and Janie Moore seems destined to always be a mystery. Clearly, she was a difficult woman to live with. Her many demands constantly interrupted Lewis's favorite occupations of reading and writing. Yet during his years with her he was extremely productive, enjoying success as an Oxford don and writing many popular and influential books, and he remained devoted and loving to her to the end of her life. He was completely secretive about the nature of the relationship, even with his brother and closest friends, and so, as Warnie wrote, it seems as though no one will ever completely understand what drew the two of them together and kept them together for more than thirty years.

Out of this difficult period in Lewis's life came the books that would bring him his greatest and most lasting fame, The Chronicles of Narnia. He claimed that their inspiration came from what he called "mental pictures" or dreams that appeared to him as early as 1914. One of them was an image of a faun walking with an umbrella and some packages in a snowy wood—the first thing Lucy sees when she enters Narnia in *The Lion, the Witch, and the Wardrobe*. Lewis took some notes in 1939, when he began making up a story to entertain some of the children who had been evacuated to the Kilns. One of these children was interested in the wardrobe there that had originally been at Little Lea. Lewis began the story with some children being evacuated to the home of a mysterious professor, but the similarities ended there, and the story moved in a different direction.

He returned to it in 1948, in the midst of dealing with Janie Moore's failing health, Warnie's increasing alcoholism, and his difficult situation at Oxford. In some ways, this was a return to the fantasy play of his childhood, and the children he originally wrote about were more like Lewis and Warnie at the turn of the century than children of the 1940s. They said things like "Crikey!" and enjoyed collecting birds' nests for a hobby. Lewis's friend Roger Lancelyn Green mentioned this to him, and he changed the characters to make them more contemporary.

The books in the Narnia series are often called Christian allegory, meaning a story that represents or interprets the Christian story. In the first book, *The Lion, the Witch, and the Wardrobe,* the great lion Aslan is killed by the evil White Witch and comes back to life, in a story that has parallels to Christ's death and resurrection. The books have been criticized for

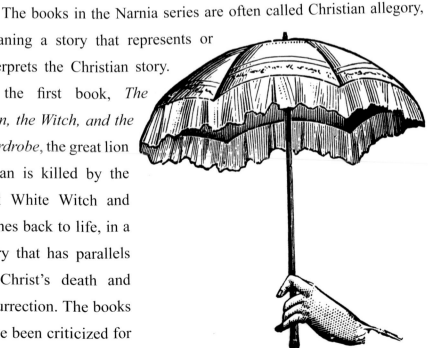

being too obviously Christian, but Lewis always denied this charge. "Everything began with images," he wrote. "A faun carrying an umbrella, a queen on a sledge, a magnificent lion. At first there wasn't even anything Christian about them; that element pushed itself in of its own accord."

So many elements of Lewis's life appear in the Narnia stories that it would be surprising if he hadn't included his Christian beliefs. Professor Kirkpatrick appears as Professor Kirke in *The Lion, the Witch, and the Wardrobe*, and the character Puddleglum is based on Fred Paxford, the pessimistic gardener who lived at the Kilns.

More important parallels appear in *The Voyage of the Dawn Treader* and *The Magician's Nephew*. Digory, the protagonist of *The Magician's Nephew*, is a child at the same time Lewis was. At the beginning of the story Digory's mother is very ill, but unlike Lewis, Digory is able to save his mother from death by bringing her a magical apple from Narnia, which restores her to good health.

In *The Voyage of the Dawn Treader*, Eustace is a despicable boy who is dragged into Narnia against his will. Eventually he is turned into a dragon and realizes how lonely his life is without the company of other humans. He tries to turn back into a boy, but is unable to do so until he meets Aslan. Aslan makes him lie on his back, then digs deep into his dragon skin, tearing it off painfully to make Eustace into a boy again, one who is kinder and more compassionate. Perhaps Lewis was thinking of his own pain when he finally surrendered to God and prayed in his room twenty years earlier.

Lewis completed *The Lion, the Witch, and the Wardrobe* at the end of 1948 and sent it to Geoffrey Bles, his publisher. The editors there weren't sure they liked it, as it was so different from anything else he had written. At this point, though, Lewis was too important of an author to turn down, so they published the work in 1950.

During the 1950s, the books were published at the rate of about one a year, although Lewis had finished writing all of them by 1954. He began an early version of *The Magician's Nephew* at the beginning of 1949, right after completing *The Lion, the Witch, and the Wardrobe*, but abandoned it and wrote *Prince Caspian* (originally titled *Drawn Into Narnia*) instead. *The Voyage of the Dawn Treader* was finished in early 1950. These were published as the second and third books in the series. Next he wrote *The Horse and His Boy*, originally titled *Narnia and the North*, which was published as the fifth Narnia book. *The Silver Chair*, which came out after *The Voyage of the Dawn Treader*, was completed in March 1951

THE CHRONICLES of NARNIA
C. S. LEWIS

THE LION, the WITCH and the WARDROBE

just after *The Lion, the Witch, and the Wardrobe* was published, which meant that five of the seven books in the series were written by the time the first book appeared to the public. Lewis finished the final Narnia book, *The Last Battle*, in 1953 and then returned to *The Magician's Nephew*, which he completed the next year.

Although the books did not get good reviews, they were immediately popular with readers. By 1956, when *The Last Battle* was published, millions of copies of all the books in The Chronicles of Narnia had been sold around the world. That year, Lewis won the Carnegie Medal, the award given annually for the best children's book published in Great Britain.

J. R. R. Tolkien was not happy with his friend's Narnia books. He felt they were sloppily written, without enough thought given to the creation of Narnia. Given that it took Tolkien twelve years to write *Lord of the Rings*, the first book in his fantasy series about Middle-Earth, this is not a surprising criticism, and in some ways it is valid. The Narnia books had many inconsistencies, which Lewis planned to revise but never did.

Tolkien's criticisms were one sign that the friendship between him and Lewis was continuing to cool. The Inklings did not survive into the 1950s. While some of the friends continued meeting at the Eagle and Child pub on Tuesday mornings, the Thursday evening gatherings ended sometime before 1950. On a Thursday in November 1949, Warnie wrote in his diary, "No Inklings tonight, so dined at home." This was the last time he mentioned the group in his diary.

The loss of Janie Moore and the fading of some friendships opened the way for one of the most important relationships of Lewis's life.

During the 1940s and 1950s, he continued his voluminous correspondence with readers from around the world. He often arranged to meet these correspondents, many of whom were women. In January 1950, he received a letter from an American woman named Joy Davidman Gresham.

She was born in New York City in 1915 to Jewish parents who had immigrated to America from Russia. Her mother, Annette, practiced Judaism and embraced the American way of life, but Joseph, her father, was an atheist and a socialist. Joy graduated from Hunter College in New York City, where she won the Bernard Cohen Short Story Prize, then went on to Columbia University, where she earned a master's degree in English literature before she was twenty-one. Following her graduation, she joined the Communist Party for a short time. Like many of her generation, she had become disillusioned with the promise of American prosperity when the Great Depression began. Joy worked as a staff writer for the Communist magazine *New Masses* and also published a book of political poems called *Letters to a Comrade*, which won the Yale Younger Poets Prize in 1938.

In 1940, Joy published a novel called *Anya* that was based on stories about Russia that her mother had told her when she was growing up. This book attracted attention from the movie industry, and she moved to Hollywood to become a screenwriter. There she met Bill Gresham, a writer who also had interests in the Communist Party. He had fought for the Communists in the Spanish Civil War during 1936, and had been in and out of psychiatric hospitals since then. He was charming and shared Joy's interests in politics and writing, and the two were married in 1942.

The couple moved to New York City, where they had two sons, David in 1944 and Douglas in 1945. In 1944, Bill's novel *Nightmare Alley* was published, and the screen rights were bought for $60,000, a huge amount for that time. This gave the Greshams enough money to move from New York City to the suburb of Pleasant Plains. Despite their good fortune, their marriage was in trouble. Bill drank too much and sometimes fired a pistol at the ceiling or threw whiskey bottles when he was drunk. In 1947, he disappeared without leaving an address or phone number, and Joy became deeply depressed. During this dark time, she felt that God appeared in her life. She described the experience as "a Person with me in the room, directly present to my consciousness—a Person so real that all my previous life was by comparison mere shadow play. And I myself was more alive than I had ever been; it was like waking up from sleep." Although this experience lasted less than a minute, it convinced Joy to convert to Christianity.

A few months later Bill reappeared, and he too became a Christian at the end of 1948, also swearing off the drinking and violence he was prone to. Unfortunately, after a few years, he began to return to his old ways. By this time, Joy had discovered the works of C. S. Lewis. After reading a few of his books, she decided to write to him at Oxford. She told a friend that she felt like she was "mentally married" to Lewis. For his part, Lewis found Joy's letter very intelligent and funny, and he wrote back to her. Their correspondence soon became a central focus of Joy's life.

In September 1952, Joy felt her marriage was beyond saving, and she decided to get away for a few months and go to England. She left her cousin Renee Pierce in charge of the house and the boys, and traveled to London. While she was there she arranged a lunch with Lewis and Warnie at one of their favorite restaurants, the Eastgate Hotel. Lewis reciprocated by inviting her to lunch at Magdalen.

Several weeks later, he invited her back to a larger lunch at Oxford where she got to meet some of his friends. Although Lewis liked her right away, some of his friends were not so impressed. When she was growing up, Joy's father had wild mood swings, making him aggressive at times. She had always tried to please him, and as a result, she could be quite aggressive herself. She often acted standoffish when she first met someone and had trouble making pleasant small talk. Since Lewis also preferred stimulating debate to chitchat, he found this a positive attribute. Some of his friends, however, were put off by what they considered rudeness.

Lewis invited Joy to the Kilns for Christmas, and she stayed there for two weeks. During her visit, she showed him a letter that she had received from Bill. He wrote that he had fallen in love with her cousin Renee, and that he hoped she could find a "real swell guy" so that he and Renee could get married.

Joy went back to New York City, but it was only to make arrangements to begin a new life in England. She divorced Bill, who did marry Renee. In April 1953, Joy and her two sons moved to London. She got the boys settled into a new school and continued writing to Lewis, visiting him occasionally in Oxford. He was somewhat wary about getting seriously involved with Joy, since he'd had trouble with women correspondents in the past. One woman had shown up at the Kilns after Lewis stopped writing to her. She was taken away by the police and later told the newspaper that she and Lewis had been secretly married. Another was arrested for making purchases posing as Lewis's wife. In jail she began to believe that they really were married, and sent a message to him that she was dying. He was kind enough to go visit her, where he discovered that she was perfectly healthy.

Because of these experiences, he proceeded cautiously, only inviting Joy to functions when he knew there would be other women around. He also was concerned about becoming too involved with a divorced woman, since the Church of England did not allow marriage after a divorce. Despite this, he definitely enjoyed being around Joy and continued to see her. He and Warnie invited the family to spend Christmas 1953 at the Kilns with them, and Lewis grew to like the boys. His years of sadness were over, and his life was taking a dramatic new turn.

Magdalen College, Oxford

# 7

## Joy

The next few years brought tremendous changes to Lewis's life. In the summer of 1954, one of his greatest academic books was published, *English Literature in the Sixteenth Century Excluding Drama*, and he was offered a professorship at Cambridge University, located about one hundred miles from Oxford. This was a newly created position specializing in the literature of the medieval and Renaissance periods, and it had been created by some of Lewis's friends at Cambridge with him in mind. If he accepted it, he would move from Magdalen College at Oxford to Magdalene College at Cambridge.

Lewis was undecided about what to do. He had always hoped to be a professor some day, and the position would free him from the tutorials he had never enjoyed. In addition, he was not popular among the Oxford faculty, and felt the Cambridge group would be more congenial. However, he felt like Oxford and the Kilns were home, and he was concerned about Warnie—his drinking problems were getting worse and Lewis knew that his brother couldn't live by himself. They considered buying a house in Cambridge, but Jack was reluctant to cut all his ties to Oxford. In the end, a compromise was reached. Lewis accepted the offer from Cambridge with the condition that he would only be in Cambridge from late Monday until early Friday. He hired a housekeeper named Molly Miller, and she and Frank Paxford—the gardener who had been at the kilns since they bought it—took care of Warnie during the week.

On November 29, 1954, Lewis's fifty-sixth birthday, he gave his inaugural lecture at Cambridge. In it, he made the claim that there was not a big cultural divide between medieval times and the Renaissance. This was an unusual belief at the time, although it has become a more common thought among scholars today. He also spoke of a divide, which he felt was far greater, between literature before the nineteenth century and modern literature. Of course, he identified himself with the older literature. His audience was impressed by his lecture, which was extremely well written and delivered, and at the end they gave him a standing ovation.

Ten days later, on December 9, his friends from Oxford gave him a farewell dinner at Merton College, where Tolkien was a professor. Many of his old friends were there, including Tolkien and his son Christopher, Nevill Coghill, Hugo Dyson, and Warnie. There was also a young man named Emrys Jones, Lewis's successor at Oxford. He had been one of Lewis's students, and had a different, quieter personality, but the same love of reading and literature. He went on to become an excellent and much-loved tutor and later a professor, remaining at Oxford for almost thirty years.

Lewis was happy at Cambridge, and he soon had many friends among the faculty. They did not seem to have the objections to his popular writings that some colleagues at Oxford had, and he continued to publish books after his move. In 1954, his autobiography, *Surprised by Joy,* was published.

Joy Gresham helped Lewis come up with the idea for his next book, *Till We Have Faces.* This work of fiction is based on the Greek myth of Cupid and Psyche, first written by the poet Apuleius in the second century A.D. The narrator is Psyche's sister, Orual. She loves her younger sister, and cannot understand Psyche's love for Cupid, who is invisible to mortals. Although Orual goes on to be a great queen, she is always bitter and jealous of Psyche's love for Cupid, which she feels destroyed her childhood relationship with her sister. At the end of her life, she is able to give her complaints to the gods and comes to understand what love really is. Lewis may have written this story with Janie Moore in mind. She was bitter about his Christian beliefs, and he always hoped she would come to understand and share them, right to the end of her life. Although Lewis considered *Till We Have Faces* his most important work of fiction, it was so different from his other books that it confused critics and was not well received.

Lewis's next book, *Reflections on the Psalms*, was written with Joy. She was also a published author, whose most recent book, *Smoke on the Mountain: An Interpretation of the Ten Commandments,* had appeared in 1954. Lewis and Joy's relationship was continuing to flourish during this time. Although she still had her own house with her two sons, she lived only about a mile from the Kilns, and was spending more and more time there. Lewis paid her rent and helped out with the boys' school fees. Because of Lewis's reticence about his personal life, it's difficult to know how he felt about her at this time. It's clear, though, that he enjoyed her company, and did not object to her frequent visits and contributions to his writing. Regardless of his feelings, he did not believe he could get married to Joy. At that time, the Church of England completely disapproved of marriage to someone who had been divorced, and would not recognize such a marriage.

Early in 1956, Lewis was forced to reconsider marrying Joy. She got the news that the British Home Office had refused to give her a permit allowing her to stay in England. The only way she could remain was to marry a British citizen. Lewis and Joy decided to have a civil marriage ceremony, which would make them legally married but would not, in Lewis's eyes, be a real marriage, since it was not performed in the church. Their wedding took place at the Oxford Registry Office on April 23, 1956. There was no fanfare, and most of their friends did not know they were married until several months later.

Joy remained in her own house, but by the fall they were making plans to move to the Kilns. During the summer, she had some pains in her leg and back that Lewis's friend Dr. Robert Havard diagnosed

Joy Gresham

as fibrositis. On October 18, at her house in Oxford, Joy got up to answer the phone, tripped over the cord, and broke her left thighbone. Doctors discovered the bone had been eaten away with cancer and that she also had cancer in her right leg, right shoulder, and left breast. She was given a fifty-fifty chance of surviving.

Lewis was now faced with a crisis. He wanted to marry Joy in the church before she died, but he knew the church would not allow it. He went to Harry Carpenter, the Bishop of Oxford, to plead his case, arguing that since Joy had married a divorced man, Bill Gresham, her first marriage shouldn't be recognized by the church. Carpenter responded that the church viewed all legal marriages as valid, even if they had taken place under different rules. He felt that allowing Lewis to get married would be worse than making such an allowance for most people. Since Lewis was such a famous Christian, his marriage would get a lot of publicity, and the church would be flooded with requests from people in similar situations.

Finally, Lewis contacted Peter Bide, a friend who had studied English literature at Oxford before World War II. Bide had become a priest and discovered that he had a gift for healing. He agreed to come to the hospital and pray for Joy's recovery, and also to officiate at their wedding. In March 1957, the doctors told Joy they had no hope for her recovery, and on March 21, Bide performed the wedding in the hospital. An announcement was published the next day in the *Times* of London, which was how most of Lewis's friends learned of this most recent marriage.

The following month, Joy came home to the Kilns to die. There was a question of what to do with her sons after her death. Bill Gresham had written that he wanted to take them back with him, but Joy was vehemently opposed to this. Lewis wrote Gresham a letter outlining Bill's shortcomings as a father and stating that he and Joy would fight in court any attempts made to get the boys. Maureen, Janie Moore's daughter, took them home with her for a while, but David, the oldest, was difficult and aggressive, and she soon returned them to the Kilns.

As the summer progressed, however, Joy seemed to be getting better. At the same time, Lewis was suffering from osteoporosis and was often in a great deal of pain. His friend Charles Williams had introduced him to the idea of substitution, in which a person can take on the suffering of someone else. Lewis came to believe that this idea was at work with him and Joy. He felt he was losing calcium from his bones at the time when she needed it most to rebuild her bones that had been ravaged by cancer. His pain subsided toward the end of 1957 as her condition began to plateau. By that time she was able to walk around with a cane, and by the Lewises' first anniversary in March 1958, the doctors could not find any trace of cancer in her bones.

This was the beginning of one of the happiest periods in Lewis's life. He told his friend Nevill Coghill, "I never expected to have, in my sixties, the happiness that passed me by in my twenties." This was as personal a remark as he ever made in terms of admitting his love for Joy and referring to his less-than-happy relationship with Janie Moore.

Joy's recovery made Warnie feel uncomfortable about staying at the Kilns. When it became clear that she was getting better, he announced that he was going to move to Ireland and find a home of his own. Lewis and Joy insisted that he stay with them. Joy tried to get him to stop drinking, but she was never successful, and he continued to go on alcoholic binges, often ending up in Our Lady of Lourdes hospital in Ireland to recover. He did, however, settle into a fairly happy routine with Joy. Later he wrote, "I decided to give the new regime a try. All my fears were dispelled. For me, Jack's marriage meant that our home was enriched and enlivened by the presence of a witty, broad-minded, well-read and tolerant Christian, whom

J. R. R. Tolkien enjoying a pipe in his study. *(Courtesy of Getty Images)*

I had rarely heard equaled as a conversationalist and whose company was a never-ending source of enjoyment."

Other Inklings, though, never warmed up to Joy. Lewis tried to re-form the group, holding meetings at the Kilns with Joy in attendance. For years, women had been excluded from meetings, and many of the married members had long suffered domestic conflicts to attend. In addition, many of Lewis's Oxford friends never felt comfortable around Joy, as she could be blunt to the point of rudeness. Some friends, like Tolkien, felt slighted that they had learned of the Lewises' marriage by reading about it in the paper. As a result, Lewis and Joy stopped socializing with most of his old friends and formed some new friendships with other couples.

Mostly, though, they enjoyed being together. They both felt that they had been given a miracle with Joy's recovery, and they treasured the time they had. In July 1958 they took a belated honeymoon to Ireland, where Joy got to meet Arthur Greeves. They flew in an airplane, a first for both of them, and returned again the next year. They also began planning a trip to Greece with their friends, Roger and June Lancelyn Green. This was an unusual step for Lewis, who hadn't been abroad since his time in the war, and had always considered travel an unnecessary extravagance. Both he and Warnie were always afraid of going to places they loved from literature, because they feared those places wouldn't live up to how they had imagined them.

In October 1959, Lewis and Joy went to the Churchill Hospital for Joy's final cancer check-up. After her years of good health and positive doctors' reports, they were both feeling optimistic and full of plans for their future. Unfortunately, their miracle had ended. The doctors told Joy that the cancer had returned and that she had, at most, a few years left to live.

Joy fought the disease through the winter, and, although she was weakening and increasingly in pain, the Lewises decided to go ahead with their trip to Greece in March 1960. They had a wonderful time, and Joy was able to see many of the places she had always wanted to visit. When they returned, however, she was nauseated and in pain for several weeks.

For the next few months, Joy was in and out of the hospital. On the morning of July 13, Warnie and Lewis were awakened by Joy's screams of pain. Lewis took her to the Radcliffe Infirmary. Warnie heard Lewis return to the Kilns at 1:40 on the morning of the fourteenth, and asked him about Joy's condition. He replied that Joy had died about twenty minutes before. Shortly before she died, Lewis said to her, "If you can—

if it is allowed—come to me when I too am on my death bed." Joy replied, "Allowed! Heaven would have a job to hold me; and as for Hell, I'd break it to bits."

Warnie, who was in charge of putting the notice of her death in the paper, had it put in the *Daily Telegraph*, which was the paper he usually read, but didn't think to put it in the much larger London *Times*. Many of their close friends, such as Roger and June Lancelyn Green, didn't even know she had died, and Joy's funeral was sparsely attended.

In 1960, Lewis published a book called *The Four Loves*. In it he explored four different kinds of love: affection, friendship, eros (romantic love), and charity (completely selfless love like the love of God). Although he had thought he knew of love before he met Joy, she taught him much about all of these kinds of love. He wrote that they had "feasted on love; every mode of it—solemn and merry, romantic and realistic, sometimes as dramatic as a thunderstorm, sometimes as comfortable and unemphatic as putting on your soft slippers." Joy's death left a hole in Lewis's life that would never be filled.

# 9

## "The Wheel Had Come Full Circle"

Douglas Gresham, Joy's son, wrote, "Jack was never again the man he had been before Mother's death. Joy had left him and also it seemed, had joy." Joy's death was the worst loss Lewis had experienced since his mother died when he was nine years old, and it changed him emotionally. Ever since the death of his mother, he had always kept his feelings hidden. Now, with Joy gone, his grief was too great to keep to himself. He frequently burst into tears, even around his friends.

Douglas Gresham found out about his mother's death when he was at boarding school in Wales. His headmaster drove him all the way back to Oxford. When Lewis saw Douglas, the two of them cried and hugged each other, Lewis comforting his stepson in a way that his own father never had been able to comfort him.

Not surprisingly, one way Lewis dealt with his grief was to write about it. The result was *A Grief Observed*, probably his most intimate and personal book, written like a diary of emotions following Joy's death. Not only did he explore his life with Joy and her death, but also the ways it had affected his faith in God. He was beginning to question the nature of God and his goodness. In one passage he wrote about God, "Go to him when your need is most desperate when all help is vain, and what do you find? A door slammed in your face and a sound of bolting and double bolting on the inside. After that, silence."

He could not, however, lose his faith after believing for almost thirty years. His perception of God changed, though, and he was no longer certain of the goodness of God. At times he thought of God as a being who set up challenges for humans to endure. He also realized that it might be impossible for people to truly understand God or his ways.

Jack sent the manuscript of *A Grief Observed* to the London publisher Faber and Faber, which was different from his usual publisher. He used the pseudonym N. W. Clerk, since he felt uncomfortable identifying himself as the author of a work that revealed such raw emotions. The managing director at Faber and Faber was the well-known poet T. S. Eliot, one of the "modern" poets that Lewis had criticized in the past. The first reader of the manuscript gave it a negative review, saying it was too morbid and might alienate readers, but Eliot felt that it had some merit, and he gave it to another reviewer for a second opinion.

By coincidence, the new reviewer was Charles Monteith, a director at the publishing house and a fellow at All Souls College at Oxford, who had studied with Lewis. He recognized Lewis's handwritten corrections on the manuscript, and he remembered that Lewis had occasionally published poetry under the pseudonym Nat Whilk, which means "I know not who" in Old English. Monteith also had heard that Lewis's wife had recently died, and he guessed correctly that Lewis was the true author of *A Grief Observed*.

When Faber and Faber learned that they had a manuscript written by C. S. Lewis, they were eager to publish it, and the book came out in 1961. Originally appearing under the pseudonym, the book sold only about 1,500 copies. After Lewis's death, Owen Barfield, Lewis's literary executor, gave permission for the book to be published with Lewis's name on it, and it went on to sell one hundred times as many copies as the first edition.

After Joy's death, Lewis continued his work at Cambridge, and he wrote another scholarly book called *An Experiment in Criticism*, published in 1961. Lewis felt there was a movement by many of the English professors at Cambridge to determine which authors their students should or shouldn't read. He believed that readers should make up their own minds about literature, and encouraged them to engage in criticism of what they read rather than simply accepting the opinions of their teachers.

He also worked on a book entitled *Letters to Malcolm: Chiefly on Prayer*, a collection of letters written to a fictional character named Malcolm. In one of the letters, Lewis refers to an earlier attempt at a book on prayer, but claims he felt inadequate to write it. By writing a collection of letters, he was able to explore different aspects of prayer without having to answer all the questions he raised. This was the last book he wrote, and it was published in 1964.

In addition to his work, Lewis still had domestic responsibilities. Warnie was drinking more than ever, following his usual routine of going to Ireland when he felt the need to drink in excess. He also was the guardian of David and Douglas Gresham, who were fourteen and fifteen years old at the time of their mother's death. David had always been independent and not particularly close to Lewis. Soon after Joy's death, he became interested in studying Judaism, and Lewis funded his studies. Since his mother had been born Jewish, David was considered

C. S. Lewis in his rooms *(Courtesy of Getty Images)*

Jewish as well, and he eventually returned to this religion. Douglas, who remained Christian, was much closer to Lewis, and Lewis wrote to Arthur that Douglas was "a bright spot" in his life.

Soon after Joy's death, Bill Gresham traveled to Oxford to see the boys. He was almost a stranger to them after so many years of living apart. Lewis and Bill's meetings were somewhat awkward due to the letters Lewis had written during Joy's illness, in which he threatened to fight Bill if he tried to get custody of the boys and pointed out Bill's shortcomings as a father. After a brief stay in Oxford, Bill returned to the United States. In 1962, he discovered he had cancer and, not wanting to suffer as Joy had, committed suicide.

In June of 1961, Lewis began to have some health problems. Arthur Greeves made a rare trip from Ireland, and during his visit told Lewis that he looked ill. After Arthur left, Lewis made an appointment for a checkup with Robert Havard, who found he had had a severely enlarged prostate and infected kidneys. Havard fitted him with a catheter to help him urinate, prescribed antibiotics, and put him on special diet. Lewis refused to give up drinking, smoking, or tea, saying he would rather live a shorter life but enjoy it.

He did take the fall term off from teaching at Cambridge, but returned in January 1962. That summer he began to have more pain, and went to a young local doctor, Tony Haines. Haines was shocked at the poor treatment Lewis had received so far. The old-fashioned catheter Dr. Havard had given him was falling apart, causing poisons to leak into Lewis's body. Haines fitted him with more modern equipment and put him on a low-protein diet, which Lewis hated, since he didn't consider a meal to be complete without a large quantity of meat.

That fall, Lewis gave a series of lectures entitled "English Literature 1300-1500," which were his last. In 1963, his only responsibility at Cambridge was supervising graduate students. That summer, as he was getting ready to leave for Ireland with Douglas Gresham, he had a heart attack during a medical exam and was put in Acland Hospital. The doctors at first thought he was dying, and a priest came to administer last rites. During the ritual, Lewis opened his eyes and asked for a cup of tea.

However, he suspected he was not going to live much longer. He had always had a great fear of death, but after Joy's death he became more accepting of it. In addition, his physical problems made life increasingly difficult. He was beginning to make peace with people and situations in his life. During the winter before his heart attack, he had a request from publishers to write a recommendation for a new book of J. R. R. Tolkien's entitled *The Adventures of Tom Bombadil*. He wrote a letter to Tolkien, saying he thought the public knew of their friendship and wouldn't believe a recommendation from him. He ended the letter, "I wish we c[oul]d ever meet," a line that inspired Tolkien's son Christopher to arrange a meeting between the two men. They got together at the Kilns, but it was awkward, and they were unable to reconcile their differences. Tolkien came to visit Lewis in the hospital after Lewis's heart attack, though.

Lewis returned to the Kilns in July. Warnie had gone on another serious drinking binge that landed him in the hospital in Ireland. A new acquaintance of Lewis's, Walter Hooper, came in to help take care of Lewis and to act as his secretary. Hooper was from the University of Kentucky, and had come to Oxford hoping to write a dissertation on Lewis.

Warnie returned in August, the same month that Lewis resigned from Cambridge University. They spent their last few months together, in the ways that had always given them the greatest pleasure, reading and talking. Warnie wrote, "The wheel had come full circle. Once again we were together in the little end room at home, shutting out from our talk the ever-present knowledge that the holidays were ending, that a new term fraught with unknown possibilities awaited us both."

On November 18, 1963, Lewis went to his last Inklings meeting at a pub called the Lamb and Flag in Oxford, which had replaced the Eagle and Child as the group's gathering place. Colin Hardie, a friend since the 1930s, was the only other person in attendance, but the two of them had an enjoyable visit.

Four days later, on November 22, Warnie brought Lewis a tray of tea in bed at about four in the afternoon. At half past five, he heard a loud crash and went upstairs to discover Lewis unconscious on the floor. A few minutes later he was dead. In the United States on the same day, President John F. Kennedy was assassinated, and the news of Lewis's death was overshadowed by that historic event.

Lewis's funeral was held at Holy Trinity Church, a short walk from the Kilns. It was attended by a small group including J. R. R. Tolkien and his son Christopher, David and Douglas Gresham, Maureen Blake, Owen Barfield, and Fred Paxton. Warnie couldn't bring himself to go, and spent the day in bed drinking. His contribution was to choose the engraving on the headstone: "Men must endure their going hence," the line from Shakespeare's *King Lear* that had been on their mother's calendar the day she died.

Following the funeral, the group gathered to hear Lewis's will read by Owen Barfield, one of the executors. Despite Lewis's success as a writer, there was just 37,772 pounds (the equivalent of seven hundred thousand pounds today). Lewis had given away most of his earnings to charity. He left money to make sure David and Douglas Gresham could complete their educations, and left the rest to Warnie, to go to David and Douglas when Warnie died. His brother also inherited the Kilns, which later went to Maureen Moore Blake. Warnie lived for nine and a half more years, mostly unhappy without Lewis, moving between the increasingly dilapidated Kilns and the homes of various friends. He died in 1973 at age seventy-seven.

During the next few decades, C. S. Lewis's estate grew enormously as his books continued selling. The Chronicles of Narnia have remained bestsellers for fifty years, selling somewhere between 50 and 100 million copies, and being translated into every major language. In 1997, the Waterstones bookstore chain and Britain's Channel 4 surveyed more than 50,000 people to make a list of the one hundred best-loved books of all time, and *The Lion, the Witch, and the Wardrobe* was rated number twenty-one (number one was Tolkien's *The Lord of the Rings*). It was the fourth most popular children's book, after *The Wind in the Willows*, *Winnie the Pooh*, and *The Hobbit*. Lewis's science fiction trilogy (*Out of the Silent Planet*, *Perelandra*, and *That Hideous Strength*) as well as *The Screwtape Letters* have all sold tens of millions of copies, and his religious books, such as *Miracles* and *Mere Christianity*, have sold hundreds of thousands and continue to be read today.

The Lewis estate has had careful managers over the years, beginning with Owen Barfield, who died in 1997 at the age of ninety-nine.

They resisted selling film rights to the books for a long time, finally agreeing to let a new company called Walden Media acquire the rights. The first movie of The Chronicles of Narnia, *The Lion, the Witch, and the Wardrobe*, was released in 2005, and its sequel *Prince Caspian* in 2008. Douglas Gresham is involved in the movies and is helping to keep them true to the books.

Over the years, some have tried to portray C. S. Lewis as a saint. The truth, though, is he was a man with many flaws. He struggled with his relationships with other people, whether they were his students, his friends, his family, or the women in his life. All his life, he searched for an elusive joy, only getting occasional glimpses of it in his reading, his religion, and his marriage. After converting to Christianity, he tried to live his life in a way that he felt God wanted him to, not always successfully. What he did succeed in doing was leaving the legacy of his writing: books that have instructed, provoked, and enchanted people for many decades and continue to reach new readers today.

# TIMELINE

**1898** Born in Belfast, Ireland, on November 29.

**1908** Mother dies of cancer.

**1916** Attends Oxford University; enlists in British Army to fight in World War I.

**1917** Rooms with Edward "Paddy" Moore; meets Moore's mother, Janie.

**1918** Wounded in the Battle of Arras; discharged from army following end of war.

**1919** Resumes studies at Oxford.

**1921** Moves in with Janie Moore and her daughter, Maureen.

**1925** Elected Fellow of Magdalen College at Oxford.

**1926** Publishes *Dymer*, an epic poem, under the name Clive Hamilton.

**1931** Re-embraces Christianity; begins incorporating religious themes into writing.

**1941** Publishes *The Screwtape Letters*; gives speeches on BBC radio about Christianity.

**1950** Publishes *The Lion, The Witch, and The Wardrobe*, first in The Chronicles of Narnia.

**1951**  Publishes *Prince Caspian*, second in The Chronicles of Narnia; Janie Moore dies.

**1952**  Publishes *The Voyage of the Dawn Treader*, third in the Chronicles of Narnia; meets Joy Gresham.

**1953**  Publishes *The Silver Chair*, fourth in The Chronicles of Narnia.

**1954**  Publishes *The Horse and His Boy*, fifth in The Chronicles of Narnia; becomes Chair of Medieval and Renaissance Literature at Cambridge.

**1955**  Publishes *The Magician's Nephew*, sixth in The Chronicles of Narnia; also publishes autobiography, *Surprised by Joy: The Shape of My Early Life*.

**1956**  Publishes *The Last Battle*, final in The Chronicles of Narnia; wins Carnegie Medal in recognition of Chronicles of Narnia; secretly marries Joy in civil ceremony.

**1960**  Joy dies.

**1961**  Publishes *A Grief Observed*, about Joy's death, under the name N. W. Clerk.

**1963**  Dies on November 22.

# Sources

### Chapter One: Warnie and Jack

p. 14    "With my mother's death . . ." C. S. Lewis, *Surprised by Joy: The Shape of My Early Life* (New York: Harcourt, Brace, and Company, 1955), 21.

p. 17    "little by little, with . . ." Ibid., 66.

p. 18    "Never, except in the front-line . . ." Ibid., 96

p. 19    "It is an amazing performance . . ." Alan Jacobs, *The Narnian: The Life and Imagination of C. S. Lewis* (New York: Harper-Collins, 2005), 36.

p. 19    "Do you not see . . ." Lewis, *Surprised by Joy*, 134.

p. 21    "I know hardly any other . . ." Jacobs, *The Narnian*, 64.

### Chapter Two: In the Trenches

p. 23    "I knew very well . . ." Lewis, *Surprised by Joy*, 183.

p. 23-24 "You may make a writer . . ." Ibid.

p. 26    "childish," Jacobs, *The Narnian,* 67.

p. 26    "I like her immensely . . ." Ibid.

p. 26    "Your boy, of course . . ." A. N. Wilson, *C. S. Lewis: A Biography* (New York: W. W. Norton and Company, 1990), 53.

p. 27    "Have arrived in Bristol . . ." Jacobs, *The Narnian*, 68.

p. 31    "I must warn the reader . . ." Lewis, *Surprised by Joy*, 198.

p. 31-32 "The thing most puzzling . . ." Jacobs, *The Narnian*, 95.

p. 33    "It was as if an . . ." Ibid., 87.

p. 33    "nightmares—or rather the same . . ." Ibid., 75.

p. 33    "I am too old . . ." Ibid.

p. 34     "All the time, but I . . ." Ibid., 80.

p. 34     "All these were rosy visions . . ." Ibid., 78.

p. 35     "Nearly all that I loved . . ." Ibid., 80.

### CHAPTER THREE: SCHOLAR

p. 37-38  "Our lives were already full . . ." Lewis, *Surprised by Joy*, 44.

p. 38     "no more pessimism, no more . . ." Ibid., 201.

p. 39     "He has read all . . ." Ibid., 199-200.

p. 46     "Elected fellow Magdalen . . ." Jacobs, *The Narnian*, 116.

p. 46     "First, let me thank . . ." Wilson, *C. S. Lewis: A Biography*, 90.

p. 47     "Very pleasant, not a cloud," Jacobs, *The Narnian*, 117.

### CHAPTER FOUR: RELUCTANT CONVERT

p. 55     "He is a smooth, pale . . ." Michael White, *C. S. Lewis: A Life* (New York: Carroll and Graf, 2004), 87.

p. 57     "the long inhibition . . ." Lewis, *Surprised by Joy*, 217.

p. 58     "I felt as if I . . ." Ibid., 225.

p. 58     "You must picture me alone . . ." Ibid., 228.

### CHAPTER FIVE: WRITE SOME OURSELVES

p. 63     "posting letters to a non-existent address . . ." Wilson, *C. S. Lewis: A Biography*, 123.

p. 63     "not precisely Christianity, tho' . . ." Jacobs, *The Narnian*, 138.

p. 64-65  "When we set out I . . ." Lewis, *Surprised by Joy*, 237.

p. 65     "I have just passed on . . ." Jacobs, *The Narnian*, 150.

p. 65     "Does this amount to a . . ." Ibid.

p. 67     "There is too little of . . ." Wilson, *C. S. Lewis*, 153.

p. 69     "It was a pleasantly ingenious . . ." Ibid., 159.

p. 70     "This is simply shocking . . ." Ibid., 157.

## CHAPTER SIX: SPEAKER OF FAITH

p. 73     "If its got to be . . ." Jacobs, *The Narnian*, 221.

p. 73     "What makes it worse . . ." Ibid.

p. 75     "Of course a war is . . ." Ibid., 222.

p. 75     "have their attention diverted . . ." Ibid.

p. 83     "dearest friend . . ." Ibid., 230.

p. 83     "the next world . . ." Ibid.

p. 83     "As if our holiday had . . ." Wilson, *C. S. Lewis: A Biography*, 205.

## CHAPTER SEVEN: CHRONICLES

p. 86     "He could be intolerant . . ." Jacobs, *The Narnian*, 265.

p. 88     "Of course, she is . . ." Ibid., 233.

p. 90     "And so ends the mysterious . . ." Wilson, *C. S. Lewis: A Biography*, 224.

p. 90     "mental pictures . . ." Ibid., 188.

p. 91-92 "Everything began with images . . ." Jacobs, *The Narnian*, 243.

p. 94     "No Inklings tonight, so . . ." Ibid., 249.

p. 96     "a Person with me in . . ." Ibid., 270.

p. 96     "mentally married . . ." Wilson, *C. S. Lewis*, 236.

p. 98     "real swell guy . . ." Ibid., 241.

## CHAPTER EIGHT: JOY

p. 106    "I never expected to have . . ." Jacobs, *The Narnian*, 279.

p. 106    "I decided to give the . . ." Ibid., 286.

p. 108    "If you can—if it is allowed . . ." Wilson, *C. S. Lewis: A Biography*, 281.

p. 108    "Allowed! Heaven would . . ." Ibid.

p. 109    "feasted on love; every . . ." Ibid., 272.

## CHAPTER NINE: "THE WHEEL HAD COME FULL CIRCLE"

p. 111    "Jack was never again . . ." Michael White, *C. S. Lewis: Creator of Narnia* (New York: Carroll and Graf, 2005), 200.

p. 112    "Go to him when your . . ." Wilson, *C. S. Lewis: A Biography*, 284.

p. 115    "a bright spot . . ." Jacobs, *The Narnian*, 331.

p. 116    "I wish we c[oul]d ever meet . . ." Wilson, *C. S. Lewis*, 294.

p. 117    "The wheel had come full . . ." Jacobs, *The Narnian*, 301.

# BIBLIOGRAPHY

Duriez, Colin. *The C. S. Lewis Chronicles*. New York: Blue-Bridge Books, 2005.

Jacobs, Alan. *The Narnian: The Life and Imagination of C. S. Lewis*. New York: HarperCollins, 2005.

Lewis, C. S. *Surprised by Joy: The Shape of My Early Life*. New York: Harcourt, Brace, and Company, 1955.

White, Michael. *C. S. Lewis: A Life*. New York: Carroll and Graf, 2004.

————. *C. S. Lewis: Creator of Narnia*. New York: Carroll and Graf, 2005.

Wilson, A. N. *C. S. Lewis: A Biography*. New York: W. W. Norton and Company, 1990.

# WEB SITES

**http://www.bbc.co.uk/religion/religions/christianity/people/cslewis_1.shtml**

This BBC (British Broadcasting Corporation) Web page features an article on C. S. Lewis that covers his childhood, conversion, marriage, and later years, along with links to related articles.

**http://www.nycslsociety.com; http://www.lewissociety.org**

There are numbers of C. S. Lewis societies. The New York C. S. Lewis Society and the C. S. Lewis Society of California are two, and both provide links to many of Lewis's works.

**http://www.time.com/time/magazine/article/0,9171,804196-1,00.html**

C. S. Lewis was featured on the cover of *Time* magazine on September 8, 1947. The inside story, titled "Don v. Devil," provides some interesting insight into the Oxford don on his home turf, and runs for seven pages on this online version of the article.

# INDEX